The Super Quick Guide to Learning Theories & Teaching Approaches

Sara Miller McCune founded SAGE Publishing in 1965 to support the dissemination of usable knowledge and educate a global community. SAGE publishes more than 1000 journals and over 800 new books each year, spanning a wide range of subject areas. Our growing selection of library products includes archives, data, case studies and video. SAGE remains majority owned by our founder and after her lifetime will become owned by a charitable trust that secures the company's continued independence.

Los Angeles | London | New Delhi | Singapore | Washington DC | Melbourne

The Super Quick Guide to Learning Theories & Teaching Approaches

Andy Goldhawk

Learning Matters
A SAGE Publishing Company
1 Oliver's Yard
55 City Road
London EC1Y 1SP

SAGE Publications Inc.
2455 Teller Road
Thousand Oaks, California 91320

SAGE Publications India Pvt Ltd
B 1/I 1 Mohan Cooperative Industrial Area
Mathura Road
New Delhi 110 044

SAGE Publications Asia-Pacific Pte Ltd
3 Church Street
#10-04 Samsung Hub
Singapore 049483

Editor: Amy Thornton
Senior project editor: Chris Marke
Cover design: Wendy Scott
Typeset by: C&M Digitals (P) Ltd, Chennai, India
Printed in the UK

Library of Congress Control Number: 2022948450

British Library Cataloguing in Publication Data

A catalogue record for this book is available from the British Library.

ISBN 978-1-5296-0579-2
ISBN 978-1-5296-0578-5 (pbk)

At SAGE we take sustainability seriously. Most of our products are printed in the UK using responsibly sourced papers and boards. When we print overseas we ensure sustainable papers are used as measured by the PREPS grading system. We undertake an annual audit to monitor our sustainability.

Contents

About the Author

Before moving into higher education Dr Andy Goldhawk was a lecturer in further education for 15 years. During this time he taught English for Speakers of Other Languages (ESOL), Spanish and IT qualifications. He was also previously a teaching and learning coach. Andy has completed a master's degree in lifelong learning and a doctorate in education. He currently works at the University of the West of England and lives in North Somerset. Andy enjoys listening to all sorts of music (usually loudly in traffic), running (slowly) and has a never-ending thirst for learning.

Acknowledgements

I want to firstly thank Amy Thornton at SAGE who believed in and championed my idea for this book from the beginning. Thank you to the design team at SAGE who produced such a vibrant design for the pages in this book. My sincere thanks also to both Professor Helen King and Dr Shaun Mudd for your valuable comments and suggestions in reviewing my manuscript, it is much appreciated. Finally, thank you Nicola, Jude and Remy for your giant hearts and endless support!

Introduction

Thank you for buying this book! I very much hope it is useful to you, whethe you are a trainee or experienced teacher, lecturer, early years practitioner, teache trainer, or anyone else whose work intersects with learning theories and teachin approaches. As a trainee teacher I often needed to quickly get my head around theory or approach to be able to discuss it, or decide where to focus my time an energy in deeper reading. This didn't stop as a teacher or as a post-grad studen As busy people, my colleagues, classmates and I sometimes wished for a source o nutshell **summaries**, written in **plain English**, that would help us **quickly grasp** th basics of a theory or approach, without having to struggle through long and comple academic papers that often use challenging language. There is the purpose of thi book: to provide a bridge to academic literature by way of concise explanation of what theories propose about learning, and the features of different teachin approaches. This is all better summed up I think in a kind message from a teache that I received on my Instagram account (@learning.theories.shared), the place started working to address this goal: 'So much of this stuff isn't discussed whe you're a trainee teacher and it should be! Making it visible like this in bite-size chunks instead of long complicated research papers means it has a much bette chance of reaching the classroom!'

Importantly, **this is not a replacement** for deeper academic reading. If you want o need to investigate a specific theory or approach more fully, use the **references** o each page (and your library search tools) to start **digging deeper** in the **academi literature**. Remember then that these summaries provide **headline information**, no detailed expositions of divergent and nuanced arguments related to each theor or approach. This book is intended to be an introduction and a **springboard** int understanding. On each page you'll find the following:

A few sentences explaining some **principal features** of the theory or approach.

A **criticism or comment** about the theory or approach. This is to help you **think critically** (see 1.5) about the theory or approach. It's important to be mindful that no theory is perfect or uncontested. All learning theories and teaching approaches are, and should be, read with a critical eye in order to judge their merits and seek out any potential weaknesses, gaps or pitfalls (and how these might be addressed).

Some suggested books and/or academic papers that can serve as a starting point for deeper reading relating to the theory or approach.

Signposting of other theories and approaches salient to the theory or approach covered on that page.

Before getting your head around different theories of learning and teaching approaches, it'll be useful to consider what we mean by '**learning**'. Page 1.1 provides a starting point for this. For the purpose of this book I draw in part from Vanlommel et al. (2018, p. 111) to define a '**teaching approach**' as 'a strategy teachers adopt when teaching' that corresponds to their underpinning assumptions of what constitutes good teaching and learning. Approaches can be **teacher-centred** in nature, meaning the intention is to transmit knowledge to students who are passive agents, or **student-centred**, where the goal is to facilitate the learning of students who are active agents in the process.

For simplicity and consistency I use the word '**teacher**' throughout this work as a **catch-all** term for anyone who in some way supports the learning of others. In reality this involves a wide range of people such as teachers, lecturers, instructors, trainers, coaches, mentors, learning consultants and parents. I use two further catch-all terms: '**student**' and '**individual**', in reference to anyone who is learning.

Vanlommel, K., Van Gasse, R., Vanhoof, J. and Petegem, P.V. (2018) 'Teachers' high-stakes decision making: how teaching approaches affect rational and intuitive data collection', *Teaching and Teacher Education*, 71, pp. 108–119.

Chapter 1:
Foundational Concepts

1.1 Learning

Learning can be defined as the **acquisition of knowledge.** Many proposed definitions of 'learning' make reference to changes in **behaviour** or changes in the **organism**. For instance, Illeris (2007, p. 3, emphasis added) describes learning as: 'any process that in living organisms leads to **permanent capacity change** and which is not solely due to biological maturation or ageing'.

There are numerous attempts at defining what learning is, many of which are criticised for being either **overly inclusive** or **not inclusive enough** in what they describe (see De Houwer et al., 2013, for a useful discussion of this).

De Houwer, J., Barnes-Holmes, D. and Moors, A. (2013) 'What is learning? On the nature and merits of a functional definition of learning', *Psychonomic Bulletin and Review*, 20(4), pp. 631–642.
Illeris, K. (2007) *How We Learn: Learning and Non-learning in School and Beyond.* London: Routledge.

1.2 Pedagogy

The art or act of teaching. This encompasses learning **theories**, **approache** **the learning environment** and **learning activities**. Pedagogical approach applied by teachers are informed by their perspectives on how learni takes place, including what the role of the teacher and the student shou be in the process.

Despite the etymology (origins) of the word, 'pedagogy' is commonly us in reference to teaching students of all ages, not solely of children.

Murphy, P. (2008) 'Defining pedagogy', in K. Hall, P. Murphy and J. Soler (eds), *Pedagog and Practice: Culture and Identities*. London: Sage, pp. 28–39.

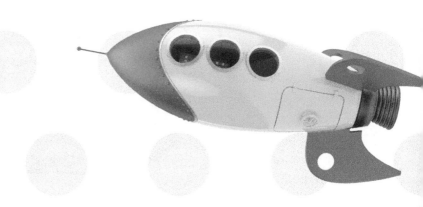

1.3 Epistemology

A branch of **philosophy** focused on the nature of, and questions relating to, **knowledge**. Classical schools of thought include:

- **Empiricism**: knowledge is gained through observation or experience. Prominent empiricists include Bertrand **Russell**, David **Hume** and John **Locke**.
- **Rationalism**: knowledge predominantly stems from reasoning. Key thinkers within this school include René **Descartes** and Baruch **Spinoza**.

Considering epistemology can help students understand how claims to knowledge are arrived at in different contexts.

Hetherington, S. (2019) *What is Epistemology?* Cambridge: Polity Press.

1.4 Metacognition

Commonly described as **'thinking about thinking'**, metacognition involves

- **self-insight**: assessing one's own thoughts and knowledge;
- **problem solving**: appraising one's own plans and processes; and
- **critical thinking**: evaluating and judging ideas.

Socratic questions (meaning questions that are deep and probing) can b
used to establish **gaps** in one's own knowledge.

Martinez, M.E. (2006) 'What is metacognition?', *Phi Delta Kappan*, 87(9), pp. 696–699.

1.5 Critical Thinking

The process of **analysing** and **evaluating** arguments to judge whether they provide sufficient **reasoning** to **act** in certain ways, or to hold particular **beliefs**. The aim of the critical thinker is to avoid doing or believing things **without** good reasons. The critical thinker aims to **recognise** their own **biases** and **errors**. **Fallacies** (mistakes in reasoning) need to be avoided.

Bowell, T., Cowan, R. and Kemp, G. (2020) *Critical Thinking: A Concise Guide*. 5th edn. Oxford: Routledge.

1.6 Reflective Practice

An **active**, **ongoing** learning **process** where the teacher deliberatel considers or **challenges** one or more aspects of their own teaching an **explores other possibilities**. New knowledge or methods can then b **tested in practice**. Reflective practice can help anchor teaching **practic** in **theory** and therefore interlink the two.

Collin, S., Karsenti, T. and Komis, V. (2013) 'Reflective practice in initial teacher training: critiques and perspectives', *Reflective Practice*, 14(1), pp. 104–117.
Dewey, J. (1933) *How We Think*. New York: Prometheus.
Schön, D. (1983) *The Reflective Practitioner: How Professionals Think in Action*. New York: Basic.

Chapter 2:

Theories of Learning

2.1 Behaviourism

Learning is demonstrated by directly observable **changes** in **behaviour**. **Learning** occurs through a process of **conditioning**, caused by interactions with a stimulus in the external environment, leading to some form of response. Principal types of conditioning include **classical** conditioning and **operant** conditioning. In the classroom, behaviourist teaching approaches (such as rote learning) involve students as passive agents who receive information transmitted to them from the teacher.

In focusing on external behaviours, behaviourism gives little attention to the role of mental (cognitive) processes, such as thoughts, reflection and the role of memory.

Pavlov, I.P. (1927) *Conditioned Reflexes: An Investigation of the Physiological Activity of the Cerebral Cortex*. London: Oxford University Press.
Skinner, B.F. (1938) *The Behaviour of Organisms: An Experimental Analysis*. New York: Appleton-Century-Crofts.
Watson, J.B. (1913) 'Psychology as the behaviorist views it', *Psychological Review*, 20(2), pp. 158–178.

Classical conditioning > p. 12
Operant conditioning > p. 13
Rote learning > p. 132
Formal learning > p. 61

2.2 Classical Conditioning

Learning happens through **association**, where two stimuli are paired together in order to **create a learned response**. For example, a dog **involuntarily** salivates on hearing a bell ring once it learns to **associate** the bell ring (stimulus 1) with the presentation of food (stimulus 2).

This has been argued to be a **reductionist**, **deterministic** explanation of behaviour that overlooks the cognitive (mental) processes that are taking place in humans and animals.

McSweeney, F.K. and Murphy, E.S. (2014) *The Wiley-Blackwell Handbook of Operant and Classical Conditioning*. Chichester: Wiley-Blackwell.
Pavlov, I.P. (1927) *Conditioned Reflexes: An Investigation of the Physiological Activity of the Cerebral Cortex*. London: Oxford University Press.
Watson, J.B. (1913). 'Psychology as the behaviorist views it', *Psychological Review*, 20(2), pp. 158–178.

Behaviourism > p. 11
Operant conditioning > p. 13

2.3 Operant Conditioning

Learning is guided by the **consequences** of **voluntary** behaviours. **Reinforcement** increases the frequency of a particular behaviour, whereas **punishment** reduces a behaviour. When a behaviour is no longer reinforced or punished, **extinction** occurs, meaning a behaviour becomes less likely. Reinforcement and punishment can both be positive or negative. For instance, a person getting burned from touching a hot stove is less likely to touch a stove in the future (this is a 'positive punishment').

As with classical conditioning, operant conditioning does not account for the role of cognition in learning; the mind is viewed as a blank canvas.

McSweeney, F.K. and Murphy, E.S. (2014) *The Wiley-Blackwell Handbook of Operant and Classical Conditioning*. Chichester: Wiley-Blackwell.
Skinner, B.F. (1938) *The Behaviour of Organisms: An Experimental Analysis*. New York: Appleton-Century-Crofts.

Behaviourism > p. 11
Classical conditioning > p. 12
Formal learning > p. 61

2.4 Cognitivism

Cognitivism focuses on the **mental processes** involved when the min
acquires, **stores** and **retrieves** information. Learning takes place a
information is drawn together in the mind to form a complete understandin
of a concept or process. The mind is sometimes described as functionin
like a computer, as it operates much like an information processor.

Some cognitivist explanations of learning have been criticised for neglectin
social and cultural influences on learning (Stuart, 2012).

Ertmer, P.A. and Newby, T.J. (1993) 'Behaviorism, cognitivism, constructivism: comparing
critical features from an instructional design perspective', *Performance Improvement
Quarterly*, 6(4), pp. 50–72.
Stuart, M. in Hunt, L. and Chalmers, D. (2012) *University Teaching in Focus: A Learning-
Centred Approach*. Oxford: Routledge.

Constructivism > p. 15
Connectivism > p. 37
Cognitive load > p. 72
Schema > p. 50
Active learning > p. 135

2.5 Constructivism

Knowledge is constructed in the mind, through **experiences** and building on **existing** knowledge. Collaborative, problem-solving tasks facilitate such learning. Different strands include:

- **cognitive** constructivism, which focuses on learning as a personal process of constructing knowledge; and
- **social** constructivism, which emphasises the social dimension and its influence in learning.

Some **unguided** forms of learning underpinned by constructivism (such as pure discovery learning) may lead to some students becoming lost in the learning process.

Piaget, J. (1957) *Construction of Reality in the Child*. London: Routledge and Kegan Paul.
Powell, K.C. and Kalina, C.J. (2009) 'Cognitive and social constructivism: developing tools for an effective classroom', *Education*, 130(2), pp. 241–250.
Vygotsky, L.S. (1978) *Mind in Society: The Development of Higher Psychological Processes*. Cambridge, MA: Harvard University Press.

Cognitivism > p. 14
Constructionism > p. 24
Discovery Learning > p. 127
Scaffolding (1) > p. 109
Assimilation > p. 17
Accommodation > p. 16

2.6 Accommodation

Learning that requires the **adjustment** of existing ideas or understanding in order to incorporate new information. Revising existing **schemata** **creating new ones** is involved in this process. Accommodation may b more **gradual** and **challenging** than its counterpart, **assimilation**. Withou accommodation, the individual would not develop.

Questions relating to accommodation (and assimilation) remain, such a when exactly the two processes occur in relation to each other.

Block, J. (1982) 'Assimilation, accommodation, and the dynamics of personality development', *Child Development*, 53(2), pp. 281–295.
Bormanaki, H.B. and Khoshhal, Y. (2017) 'The role of equilibration in Piaget's theory of cognitive development and its implication for receptive skills: a theoretical study', *Journal Language Teaching and Research*, 8(5), pp. 996–1005.
Hanfstingl, B., Arzenšek, A., Apschner, J. and Gölly, K.I. (2021) 'Assimilation and accommodation: a systematic review of the last two decades', *European Psychologist*, pp. 1–18. Available at: http://dx.doi.org/10.1027/1016-9040/a000463
Piaget, J. (1957) *Construction of Reality in the Child*. London: Routledge and Kegan Paul.

Cognitivism > p. 14
Constructivism > p. 15
Schema > p. 50
Assimilation > p. 17
Cognitive dissonance > p. 71

2.7 Assimilation

Assimilation occurs when new information fits into (rather than adjusts) a student's **existing** frameworks (or **schemata**) of ideas and understandings of a phenomenon. This means new information adds to the individual's existing understanding of a concept. Assimilation can be **quicker** and less challenging than its counterpart, **accommodation**.

Questions relating to assimilation (and accommodation) remain, such as when exactly the two processes occur in relation to each other.

Block, J. (1982) 'Assimilation, accommodation, and the dynamics of personality development', *Child Development*, 53(2), pp. 281–295.
Hanfstingl, B., Arzenšek, A., Apschner, J. and Gölly, K.I. (2021) 'Assimilation and accommodation: a systematic review of the last two decades', *European Psychologist*, pp. 1–18. Available at: http://dx.doi.org/10.1027/1016-9040/a000463
Piaget, J. (1957) *Construction of Reality in the Child*. London: Routledge and Kegan Paul.

Cognitivism > p. 14
Constructivism > p. 15
Schema > p. 50
Assimilation > p. 17

2.8 Zone of Proximal Development

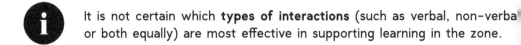 Within the zone of proximal development (ZPD) knowledge is constructed through **social interactions** with '**more knowledgeable others**' such as teachers, parents or peers. The ZPD is the space between a student's current knowledge level and their potential level. The zone is dynamic and represents learning as a **continual**, **lifelong** process; once an individual learns with the support of others, the zone shifts to the next point of learning.

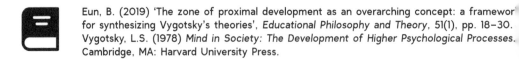 It is not certain which **types of interactions** (such as verbal, non-verbal or both equally) are most effective in supporting learning in the zone.

Eun, B. (2019) 'The zone of proximal development as an overarching concept: a framework for synthesizing Vygotsky's theories', *Educational Philosophy and Theory*, 51(1), pp. 18–30.
Vygotsky, L.S. (1978) *Mind in Society: The Development of Higher Psychological Processes*. Cambridge, MA: Harvard University Press.

Constructivism > p. 15
Scaffolding (1) > p. 109
Coaching and mentoring > p. 87

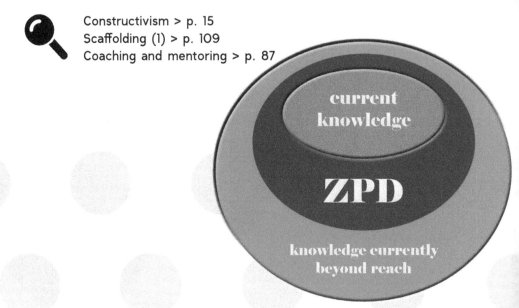

current knowledge

ZPD

knowledge currently beyond reach

2.9 Humanist education

 A **student-centred** theory that encompasses the **whole** person. Learning content needs to be relevant to students' own **interests** and **concerns**, and students require a degree of **control** over their own learning. This means student choice over learning goals, activities and the materials they are using to learn. The teacher **facilitates** learning; self-evaluation is more useful than testing and grades. Some educational approaches draw on these humanistic elements, such as **Montessori**, **Steiner** and **Reggio Emilia**.

 A **potential** concern of humanistic education is that **it views testing and grades as not useful**.

Maslow, A. (1987) *Motivation and Personality*. 3rd edn. New York: Harper and Row.
Rogers, C. (1994) *Freedom to Learn*. New York: Prentice Hall.

Montessori > p. 43
Steiner education > p. 45
Reggio Emilia > p. 44
Andragogy > p. 20
Hierarchy of needs > p. 25

2.10 Andragogy

 The act of teaching specifically **adult** students, underpinned by a set of **assumptions** (about adults) that need to inform the planning and teaching of adults, in order for **effective** learning to occur. The assumptions include

- the **need to know** why something is important to learn;
- adults' self-concept: adults are **autonomous** and **independent**;
- adults learn from a rich array of **life experiences**;
- adults are **inherently ready** to learn;
- adults are **internally motivated** to learn;
- an orientation to learning: what adults learn is for immediate, rather than future use.

 Critics argue that adult and child learning is **more similar** than these assumptions infer.

 Knowles, M.S. (1980) *The Modern Practice of Adult Education: From Pedagogy to Andragogy*. 2nd edn. New York: Cambridge.
Merriam, S.B. and Baumgartner, L. (2020) *Learning in Adulthood: A Comprehensive Guide*. 4th edn. San Francisco: Jossey-Bass.

 Humanist education > p. 19
Pedagogy > p. 4
Andragogy vs pedagogy > p. 21

The Super Quick Guide to Learning Theories and Teaching Approaches

2.11 Andragogy vs pedagogy

Some principal differences in adult and child learning according to andragogy:

Andragogy	Pedagogy
The purpose of learning is to **apply knowledge** through tasks and **problem solving**	The focus is on gaining knowledge in order to **advance** to the **next level** or **stage**
The student is **self-directed**, **autonomous** and responsible for their own learning	The **teacher** is **responsible** for what is taught
Motivation to learn derives from **within the individual**	The individual is motivated by **external pressures** and **rewards**
Adult students can draw on **life experiences** and **existing knowledge** in the learning process	Child students bring **little experience** to the learning process

2.12 Heutagogy

Learning that is **self-determined** and **transformative**. Heutagogy emphasise self-directed action, **reflection** and the **learning process** itself. Student have **autonomy** and **agency** over the learning process (meaning what ar how they will learn) which offers good preparation for operating in th workplace. This approach can lead to strong student engagement and deep(er) understanding of the learning content. The teacher's role is **guide**, **coach** and **mentor**.

Literature on heutagogy has grown since the turn of the 21st centur and describes a shift in control of learning to students themselves

Abraham, R. R. and Komattil, R. (2017) 'Heutagogic approach to developing capable learners', *Medical Teacher*, 39(3), pp. 295-299. Available at: http://dx.doi.org/10.1080/C 42159X.2017.1270433
Hase, S. and Kenyon, C. (2000) 'Heutagogy: a child of complexity theory', *Complicity: An International Journal of Complexity and Education*, 4(1), pp. 111–117.
Moore, R.L. (2020) 'Developing lifelong learning with heutagogy: contexts, critiques, and challenges', *Distance Education*, 41(3), pp. 381–401.

Humanist education > p. 19
Constructivism > p. 15
Active learning > p. 135
Coaching and mentoring > p. 87

2.13 Critical Pedagogy

Core tenets of critical pedagogy are that teaching is an inherently **political** act and **emancipation** should be central. Students are **active** agents who apply **critical thinking** and produce their **own knowledge**. The teacher and the students are regarded as **equals**. **Praxis** (meaning a process of **reflection** and taking **action** against oppression) plays an important role.

A concern of critical pedagogy is that it could itself be perceived as authoritarian, in that it gives radical educators **authority to decide** who are the oppressed, and how and when this oppression should be addressed (Yagelski, 2006).

Freire, P. (1970) *Pedagogy of the Oppressed*. New York: Herder and Herder.
Yagelski, R. (2006) 'Review: radical to many in the educational establishment: the writing process movement after the hurricanes', *College English*, 68(5), pp. 531–544.

Dogme > p. 77
Dialogic pedagogy > p. 113
Critical thinking > p. 7

2.14 Constructionism

Overlapping with, but differing from, constructivism. Meaningful learning takes place through students **constructing tangible products** or objects that solve real-world problems. The products are then shared (at various stages of construction), compared and critiqued, with students' discussion facilitating knowledge construction. A **collaborative** learning environment helps to enable this active learning approach.

Constructionism therefore describes learning as a collaborative process. See Mohammad and Farhana (2018) for a useful discussion comparing constructionism and constructivism.

Ames, M. (2018) 'Hackers, computers, and cooperation: a critical history of logo and constructionist learning', *Proceedings of the ACM on Human-Computer Interaction*, 2, pp. 1–19.
Mohammad, R. and Farhana, R. (2018) 'Dilemma between constructivism and constructionism', *Journal of International Education in Business*, 11(2), pp. 273–290.
Papert, S. and Harel, I. (1991) *Constructionism*. New York: Ablex.

Constructivism > p. 15
Problem-based learning > p. 28
Active learning > p. 135
Maker education > p. 124

2.15 Hierarchy of Needs

Learning is affected by the extent to which **physiological** and other needs are being met in any moment. Once **lower order** (or **'deficit'**) **needs** are met, individuals can attend to **higher order** needs, such as self-actualisation. Abraham Maslow (who developed the hierarchy), suggested that a tier **doesn't** need to be met fully before the next tier of the hierarchy can be reached. The hierarchy is commonly shown in a pyramid, as on this page; however, Maslow himself did not use a pyramid to illustrate his hierarchy.

People can live in poor conditions where some physiological needs are not met, yet still experience friendship and accomplishment.

Maslow, A.H. (1943) 'A theory of human motivation', *Psychological Review*, 50(4), pp. 370–396.
Maslow, A.H. (1962) *Toward a Psychology of Being*. Princeton, NJ: D. Van Nostrand.
Maslow, A.H. (1987) *Motivation and Personality*. 3rd edn. Delhi: Pearson Education.

Humanist education > p. 19
Pedagogy > p. 4

Personal accomplishment

Esteem
(accomplishment)

Belonging
(friendship, family)

Safety
(security, health)

Physiological
(air, food, shelter)

2.16 Bloom's Taxonomy

A **taxonomy** of **cognitive** processes that can help when designing learning objectives. Lower levels need to be achieved before higher levels can be reached, meaning that **foundational** knowledge precedes **higher order** learning. This taxonomy has been revised since its initial development in 1956, with words changed in the taxonomy in order to tweak or clarify the concepts initially proposed (the original taxonomy is illustrated on this page).

The taxonomy may infer that there is a hierarchy of importance regarding these cognitive processes, leading to lower levels being neglected.

Anderson, L.W. (ed.), Krathwohl, D.R. (ed.), Airasian, P.W., Cruikshank, K.A., Mayer, R.E., Pintrich, P.R., Raths, J. and Wittrock, M.C. (2001) *A Taxonomy for Learning, Teaching, and Assessing: A Revision of Bloom's Taxonomy of Educational Objectives* (complete edn). New York: Longman.
Bloom, B.S. (ed.), Engelhart, M.D., Furst, E.J., Hill, W.H. and Krathwohl, D.R. (1956) *Taxonomy of Educational Objectives: The Classification of Educational Goals. Handbook 1: Cognitive Domain.* New York: David McKay.

Constructivism > p. 15
Scaffolding 1 > p. 109
Deep and surface learning > p. 33

Evaluation

Synthesis

Analysis

Application

Comprehension

Knowledge

2.17 Experiential Learning

Learning takes place through a process of direct **experience**, **reflection** and **meaning-making**. It can take place independently or with facilitation. A cyclical process (or 'learning cycle') of four stages is proposed (Kolb, 1984):

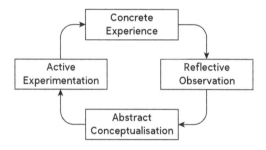

This cycle has been considered overly simplistic and formulaic, inferring that an individual must proceed through each stage in order for learning to occur, when this may not always be the case.

Dewey, J. (1938) *Experience and Education*. New York: Kappa Delta.
Kolb, D.A. (1984) *Experiential Learning: Experiences as the Source of Learning and Development*. New Jersey: Prentice Hall.
Moon, J. (2013) *A Handbook of Reflective and Experiential Learning: Theory and Practice*. Oxford: Routledge.

Active learning > p. 135
Constructivism > p. 15
Epistemology > p. 5
Enquiry learning > p. 117

2.18 Problem-based Learning

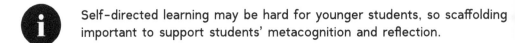 Students learn by analysing and solving **authentic problems**. A proble[m] functions as the **stimulus** for the development and application of variou[s] skills, including: problem solving, critical thinking, reasoning, collaboratio[n] and reflection. This **self-directed** learning tends to involve working in sm[all] groups, in which debate and discussion fosters **higher order** thinking an[d] the shared construction of knowledge. In problem-based learning (PB[L]) the teacher acts as **facilitator**.

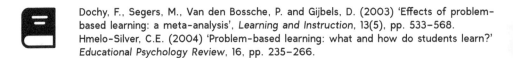 Self-directed learning may be hard for younger students, so scaffolding [is] important to support students' metacognition and reflection.

Dochy, F., Segers, M., Van den Bossche, P. and Gijbels, D. (2003) 'Effects of problem-based learning: a meta-analysis', *Learning and Instruction*, 13(5), pp. 533–568.
Hmelo-Silver, C.E. (2004) 'Problem-based learning: what and how do students learn?' *Educational Psychology Review*, 16, pp. 235–266.

Constructivism > p. 15
Critical thinking > p. 7
Bloom's taxonomy > p. 26
Metacognition > p. 6
Facilitation > p. 116
Scaffolding (1) > p. 109

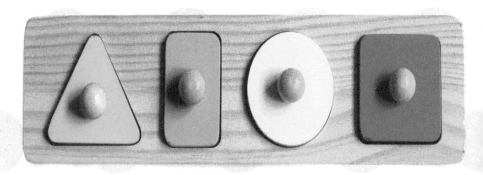

2.19 Situated Learning and Communities of Practice

Knowledge is co-constructed in **authentic** contexts where individuals can engage with **real-world problems**. Newcomers learn from others in a **community of practice** (a group of people who are **active practitioners** in a particular field of work or who share a **common goal**) through 'legitimate peripheral participation'. In doing so newcomers move from the periphery to become **full practitioners** in the community.

Legitimate peripheral participation is not intended to describe a teaching technique, rather a means to understand learning as a social process.

Kakavelakis, K. and Edwards, T. (2012) 'Situated learning theory and agentic orientation: a relational sociology approach', *Management Learning*, 43(5), pp. 475–494.
Lave, J. and Wenger, E. (1991) *Situated Learning: Legitimate Peripheral Participation*. Cambridge: Cambridge University Press.

Constructivism > p. 15
Social learning > p. 35
Active learning > p. 135
Experiential learning > p. 27

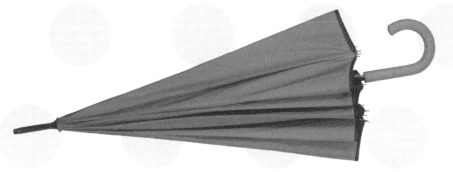

2.20 Sensory Theory

When the **five senses** are stimulated and involved, effective learning results. Knowledge is predominantly acquired through **seeing** (75 per cent) followed by **hearing** (13 per cent). The involvement of visual elements in learning activities is therefore recommended. **Multi-sensory** experiences incur the greater learning.

In attempting to adhere to this theory, imaginative approaches to teaching could be required for some theoretical disciplines where involving many of the senses would be tricky.

Laird, D. (1985) *Approaches to Training and Development*. Reading, MA: Addison-Wesley.

Active learning > p. 135
Multiple intelligences > p. 49
Learning styles > p. 51

2.21 Visible Learning

Hattie (2009) identified 138 variables that affect learning outcomes (a number that later increased). A positive impact on outcomes occurs through, for instance: students' **self-reported** grades; **formative evaluation**; and **teacher clarity**. Outcomes are also negatively impacted by various factors, such as **boredom** and a **lack of sleep**. The greatest effects occur when teachers see learning from the perspective of their students, and students develop into their own teachers.

Concerns have been expressed relating to both the methodology used by Hattie and his conceptualisation of 'learning'.

Hattie, J. (2009) *Visible Learning: A Synthesis of Over 800 Meta-Analyses Relating to Achievement*. New York: Routledge.
Hattie, J. (2012) *Visible Learning for Teachers: Maximizing Impact on Learning*. London: Routledge.
Larson, S.N (2018) 'Blindness in seeing: a philosophical critique of the visible learning paradigm in education', *Education Sciences*, (9)1, pp. 1–12.
Rømer, T.A. (2019) 'A critique of John Hattie's theory of visible learning', *Educational Philosophy and Theory*, (51)6, pp. 587–598.

Reflective practice > p. 8
Assessment for learning > p. 95
Constructivism > p. 15
Learning > p. 3
Non-learning > p. 67

2.22 Play-based Learning

Children learn through play. Play-based learning can be located on continuum according to the level of adult involvement in play, between:

- **free play**: child-directed, spontaneous, intrinsically motivated pla which can facilitate the development of self-regulation, problem solving and social competence; and
- **guided play**: teacher-directed or mutually directed play that can a the development of academic skills; learning opportunities are pur posefully incorporated into play.

This is just one description of play-based learning. Bubikova-Moan et a (2019) note there is **no consensus definition** of this form of learning.

Bubikova-Moan, J., Hjetland, H.N. and Wollscheid, S. (2019) 'ECE teachers' views on play-based learning: a systematic review', *European Early Childhood Education Research Journa* (27)6, pp. 776–800.
Pyle, A. and Danniels, E. (2017) 'A continuum of play-based learning: the role of the teacher in play-based pedagogy and the fear of hijacking play', *Early Education and Development*, 28(3), pp. 274–289.

Active learning > p. 135
Outdoor learning > p. 123
Discovery learning > p. 127
Experiential learning > p. 27
Scaffolding (1) > p. 109

2.23 Deep and Surface Learning

With deep learning, students are intrinsically motivated to understand underlying **principles**, detect **patterns** and seek **meaning**. **Critical thinking** is applied to new learning content, with **links** made between new ideas and prior knowledge. **Surface learning** involves rote learning, memorisation and the passive acceptance of information, usually with the aim of passing a test.

These terms may lead to the idea that students are either deep or surface learners as an inherently fixed characteristic.

Alt, D. and Boniel-Nissim, M. (2018) 'Links between adolescents' deep and surface learning approaches, problematic internet use, and fear of missing out (FoMO)', *Internet Interventions: The Application of Information Technology in Mental and Behavioural Health*, 13, pp. 30–39.
Dolmans, D., Loyens, S., Marcq, H. and Gijbels, D. (2016) 'Deep and surface learning in problem-based learning: a review of the literature', *Advances in Health Sciences Education*, 21(5), pp. 1087–1112.
Howie, P. and Bagnall, R. (2013) 'A critique of the deep and surface approaches to learning model', *Teaching in Higher Education*, 18(4), pp. 389–400.

Constructivism > p. 15
Metacognition > p. 6
Critical thinking > p. 7
Concept-based learning > p. 128
Rote learning > p. 132

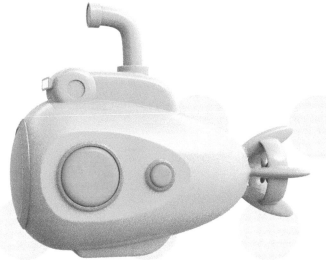

2.24 Insight Learning

This theory derives from **gestalt** psychology, 'Gestalt' meaning form shape. Rather than arriving at solutions through trial and error, insigl learning involves **reflecting** on (internal representations of) a proble **situation**, resulting in **instant** new understandings through a sudde insight (or, a 'flash of inspiration') of the solution. Insight occurs throug individuals **making associations** between objects and/or actions that lea to a solution.

Behaviourists argue that insight is not sudden and suggest that prio reinforcement is involved in this process.

Ash, I.K., Jee, B.D. and Wiley, J. (2012) 'Investigating insight as sudden learning', *The Journal of Problem Solving*, 4(2), pp. 1–27.
Köhler, W. (1959) 'Gestalt psychology today', *American Psychologist*, 14, pp. 727–734.
Windholz, G. and Lamal, P.A. (1985). 'Koehler's insight revisited', *Teaching of Psychology*, 1 pp. 165–167.

Cognitivism > p. 14
Metacognition > p. 6
Problem-based learning > p. 28
Discovery learning > p. 127
Enquiry learning > p. 117

2.25 Social Learning

Learning resulting from individuals **observing** and **imitating** others' behaviours and emotional **reactions**. **Role models** (such as peers, family or teachers) therefore have an **important** role in this form of learning. Further, people learn from seeing others being **rewarded** or **punished** for particular behaviours. Learning can also take place through individuals' active social participation in a community of practice.

It cannot be taken for granted that such participation will guarantee (social) learning will occur.

Bandura, A. (1977) *Social Learning Theory*. New York: General Learning Press.
Lave, J. and Wenger, E. (1991) *Situated Learning: Legitimate Peripheral Participation*. Cambridge: Cambridge University Press.
Reed, M.S., Evely, A.C., Cundill, G., Fazey, I., Glass, J., Laing, A., Newig, J., Parrish, B., Prell, C., Raymond, C. and Stringer, L.C. (2010) 'What is social learning'? *Ecology and Society*, 15(4). Available at: https://www.ecologyandsociety.org/vol15/iss4/resp1/

Cognitivism > p. 14
Situated learning > p. 29
Operant conditioning > p. 13
Situated learning and Communities of Practice > p. 29

2.26 Learning Pyramid

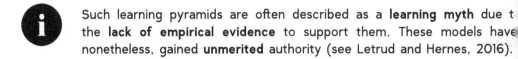

Different **learning modes** (such as hearing, talking and doing) lead t[o] differing levels of **retention** of learning content, as illustrated in the diagra[m] on this page (this specific pyramid was proposed by Dale, 1954). This an[d] other models indicate that learning by doing leads to the highest retentio[n] rates, while reading or listening leads to the lowest levels of retention.

Such learning pyramids are often described as a **learning myth** due t[o] the **lack of empirical evidence** to support them. These models have nonetheless, gained **unmerited** authority (see Letrud and Hernes, 2016).

Dale, E. (1954) *Audio-visual Methods in Teaching*. 2nd edn. New York: Holt-Dryden.
Letrud, K. and Hernes, S. (2016) 'The diffusion of the learning pyramid myths in academia: an exploratory study', *Journal of Curriculum Studies*, 48(3), pp. 291–302.

Active learning > p. 135
Sensory theory > p. 30
Experiential learning > p. 27
Formal learning > p. 61

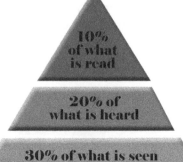

10% of what is read

20% of what is heard

30% of what is seen

50% of what is heard and seen

70% of what is said and written

90% of what is said as an activity is completed

2.27 Connectivism

Learning resides not solely within individuals, but (also) in **organisations** and **databases**, and occurs through a process of **connecting information** from differing sources. This theory considers (therefore) the **impact of technologies** on learning. Connectivist learning involves **up-to-date** knowledge and incorporates a range of opinions.

There are differing perspectives as to whether connectivism constitutes a learning theory. See Kop and Hill (2008) for a comprehensive discussion relating to this question.

Kop, R. and Hill, A. (2008) 'Connectivism: learning theory of the future or vestige of the past?', *International Review of Research in Open and Distance Learning*, (9)3, pp. 1–13. Siemens, G. (2005) 'Connectivism: learning as network creation', *International Journal of Instructional Technology and Distance Learning*, pp. 1–9. Available at: https://jotamac. typepad.com/jotamacs_weblog/files/Connectivism.pdf

Learning > p. 3
Epistemology > p. 5
Situated learning > p. 29

2.28 Spiral Curriculum

The basic ideas of a topic or subject can be taught even at a young age (or during the early stages of a curriculum). These ideas are **revisited** at later stages of the curriculum, with the aim of both consolidating and **extending** learning. This means rather than solely being repetition, each visit **builds complexity** and **depth** to what is being learned. Scaffolding may be gradually **removed** each time a topic is revisited.

The spiral curriculum has been claimed to hinder learning in its (claimed) **superficial treatment** of topics and the speed at which new concepts are introduced (see Snider, 2004).

Bruner, J. (1977) *The Process of Education*. 2nd edn. Cambridge, MA: Harvard University Press.
Gibbs, B.C. (2014) 'Reconfiguring Bruner: compressing the spiral curriculum', *Phi Delta Kappan*, 95(7), pp. 41–44.
Snider, V.E. (2004) 'A comparison of spiral versus strand curriculum', *Journal of Direct Instruction*, 4(1), pp. 29–39.

Constructivism > p. 15
Scaffolding (1) > p. 109
Discovery learning > p. 127
Bloom's taxonomy > p. 26
Mastery learning > p. 130

2.29 Threshold Concepts

A concept that leads to a **fundamental shift** in understanding that is required for progression. A threshold concept has also been termed a **'conceptual gateway'**. Mayer and Land (2003) offer the example of a threshold concept in cooking being heat transformation. In contrast are **'core concepts'**, which are conceptual building blocks that **do not** lead to a fundamental shift in understanding of the subject.

Critics question the definition of a 'threshold concept' and claim it is very difficult to identify such concepts.

Meyer, J.H.F. and Land, R. (2003) 'Threshold concepts and troublesome knowledge: linkages to thinking and practice within the disciplines', *ETL Project*, Occasional Report 4. Available at: http://www.etl.tla.ed.ac.uk/docs/ETLreport4.pdf
Rowbottom, D.P. (2007) 'Demystifying threshold concepts', *Journal of Philosophy of Education*, 41(2), pp. 263–270.
Salwén, H. (2021) 'Threshold concepts, obstacles or scientific dead ends?', *Teaching in Higher Education*, 26(1), pp. 36–49.

Learning > p. 3
Schema > p. 50
Accommodation > p. 16
Cognitive dissonance > p. 71

Chapter 3:
Educational Frameworks

3.1 Montessori

An approach that seeks to educate **the senses** and foster **independence**. Particular features include: **mixed-age** classrooms; **student choices** of activity (with limits); a relaxed, low anxiety learning **environment**; no tests; and a **discovery approach** to learning. The teacher **collaborates** with the children and **facilitates** (rather than leads) their learning. Assessment takes place through ongoing evaluation and qualitative notes taken for each child.

It has been suggested that Montessori education remains somewhat on the margins, as this approach differs somewhat from conventional education (such as students grouped according to age, and the teacher delivering information to students).

Lillard, A.S. (2019) 'Shunned and admired: Montessori, self-determination, and a case for radical school reform', *Educational Psychology Review*, 31(4), pp. 939–965.
Montessori, M. (1964) *Montessori Method*. New York: Schocken.
O'Donnell, M. (2013) *Maria Montessori: a critical introduction to key themes and debates*. London: Bloomsbury Academic.

Sensory theory > p. 30
Discovery learning > p. 127
Facilitation > p. 116
Humanist education > p. 19
Zone of proximal development > p. 18

3.2 Reggio Emilia

An **experiential** approach to learning in which young children:

- are **active co-constructors** of knowledge;
- require some **control** over their own learning;
- need wide-ranging **opportunities** to **express** themselves.

Expression takes place through **'a hundred languages'** (such as writing, movement and construction). The environment is the **'third teacher'**, which is arranged to facilitate relationships across the school community. Learning takes place through investigations and projects, and teachers document learning through project work, photos or videos.

Various concerns have been raised about the documentation process, including the role of teachers' subjectivity: one teacher may perceive different learning or meaning within a student's work as compared with another teacher.

Matusov, E., Marjanovic-Shane, A. and Meacham, S. (2016) 'Pedagogical voyeurism: dialogic critique of documentation and assessment of learning', *International Journal of Educational Psychology*, 5(1), pp. 1–26.
New, R.S. (2007) 'Reggio Emilia as cultural activity theory in practice', *Theory into Practice*, 46(1), pp. 5–13.
Senent, I.G., Kelley, K. and Abo-Zena, M.M. (2021) 'Sustaining curiosity: Reggio-Emilia inspired learning', *Early Child Development and Care*, 191(7–8), pp. 1247–1258.

Constructivism > p. 15
Discovery learning > p. 127
Experiential learning > p. 27
Humanist education > p. 19

3.3 Steiner Education

An experiential approach that takes into account the whole child. Artistic elements are important to foster imagination and creativity, and modern media is avoided. Teachers stay with their groups for several years. The curriculum features the geographical and cultural location of the school and the outdoors is embraced as an additional setting for learning. The developmental stages are: birth–seven (involving play and imitation); seven–14 (with hands-on learning); and 14–21 (with 'intellectual stimulation').

A concern is that Steiner education is informed by 'anthroposophy', a spiritual philosophy that some have called pseudoscientific.

Sobo, E.J. (2014) 'Play's relation to health and well-being in preschool and kindergarten: a Waldorf (Steiner) education perspective', *International Journal of Play*, 3(1), pp. 9–23.
Ullrich, H., Duke, J. and Balestrini, D. (2014) *Rudolf Steiner*. London: Bloomsbury.

Constructivism > p. 15
Experiential learning > p. 27
Active learning > p. 135
Humanist education > p. 19

3.4 Home Schooling

Education of children that is conducted at home, rather than in a school environment. Materials and other resources already at home can be used for learning, such as games and food. This approach can foster self-awareness, inquisitiveness and an egalitarian attitude.

Structured home schooling involves teaching and learning that follows a specified curriculum.

An **unschooling** approach is child-led, with learning taking place through play or other hands-on, spontaneous experiences.

There is mixed evidence of the effectiveness of home schooling.

Lubienski, C., Puckett, T. and Jameson Brewer, T. (2013) 'Does homeschooling "work"? A critique of the empirical claims and agenda of advocacy organizations', *Peabody Journal of Education*, (88)3, pp. 378–392.

Neuman, A. and Guterman, O. (2016) 'The clash of two world views: a constructivist analysis of home educating families' perceptions of education', *Pedagogy, Culture and Society*, 24(3), pp. 359–369.

Ray, B.D. (2017) 'A systematic review of the empirical research on selected aspects of homeschooling as a school choice', *Journal of School Choice*, 11(4), pp. 604–621.

Constructivism > p. 15
Active learning > p. 135
Play-based learning > p. 32

Chapter 4:

Brain Based Theories

4.1 Multiple Intelligences

Humans possess **various types** of **intelligence** corresponding to different contexts. Individuals' intellectual **capacity** in each context **differs** and may relate to experience or genetics. Types of intelligence include: **linguistic**, **kinaesthetic** (relating to movement), **interpersonal**, **musical**, **logical-mathematical**, **spacial** (perceiving the visual world), **intrapersonal** (self-awareness) and **naturalist** (understanding the natural world).

Critics suggest that these different intelligences amount to differing manifestations of general intelligence.

Gardner, H. (1993) *Frames of Mind: The Theory of Multiple Intelligences.* 2nd edn. London: Fontana.
Shearer, C.B. and Karanian, J.M. (2017) 'The neuroscience of intelligence: empirical support for the theory of multiple intelligences?', *Trends in Neuroscience and Education*, 6, pp. 211–223.

Learning styles > p. 51
Neuroeducation > p. 52

4.2 Schema (*pl.* schemata)

A cognitive **framework** that organises **existing knowledge** relating to a specific aspect of the world (such as an object or a concept). **New information** either adds to a schema (see: **assimilation**) or leads to the formation of a new schema (see: **accommodation**). Accommodation can be more gradual and challenging than assimilation, as new information that does not add to an existing schema may conflict with existing information, leading to **cognitive dissonance**. Schemata are also described as **mental structures** or **units of knowledge**.

The term 'schema' has been defined in different ways by different people. The concept as set out above summarises how it was used by Jean Piaget (1952).

Piaget, J. (1952) *The Origins of Intelligence in Children*. New York: International Universities Press.
Plant, K.L. and Stanton, N.A. (2013) 'The explanatory power of schema theory: theoretical foundations and future applications in ergonomics', *Ergonomics*, 56(1), pp. 1–15.

Cognitivism > p. 14
Constructivism > p. 15
Assimilation > p. 17
Accommodation > p. 16
Cognitive dissonance > p. 71

4.3 Learning Styles

Individuals can be **categorised** as (for instance) visual, auditory or kinaesthetic learners, and learning activities need to be **tailored** to accommodate such preferences. Numerous learning styles models have been proposed, for instance Honey and Mumford (1992) claim that individuals fall into one of four categories according to their learning preferences: 'activist', 'theorist', 'pragmatist' or 'reflector'.

There is widespread criticism in the literature that teaching based on such categories **does not** result in improved learning. This theory has been called a **'neuromyth'** for its **lack** of supporting evidence (for instance see Dekker et al., 2012).

Coffield, F., Moseley, D., Hall, E. and Ecclestone, K. (2004) *Learning Styles and Pedagogy in Post-16 Learning: A Systematic and Critical Review*. London: Learning and Skills Research Centre.

Dekker, S., Lee, N.C., Howard-Jones, P. and Jolles, J. (2012) 'Neuromyths in education: prevalence and predictors of misconceptions among teachers', *Frontiers in Psychology*, 429, pp. 1–8.

Honey, P. and Mumford, A. (1992) *The Manual of Learning Styles*. 3rd edn. Maidenhead: Peter Honey.

Rogowsky, B.A., Calhoun B.M. and Tallal, P. (2020) 'Providing instruction based on students' learning style preferences does not improve learning', *Frontiers in Psychology*, 11, p. 164.

Multiple intelligences > p. 49
Sensory theory > p. 30
Neuroeducation > p. 52

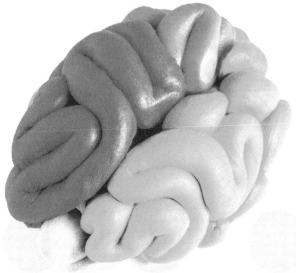

4.4 Neuroeducation

An emergent field that brings together **education** and **neuroscienc** (among other disciplines), with the goal of informing education policy an practice. Studies of memory, for example, can inform our understandin of how we learn. Learning can also affect the brain: learning to read, fo instance, alters brain activation patterns.

A challenge to neuroeducation is that of **neuroscientists** and **educationa researchers** understanding one another's disciplines, with the potentia for misunderstandings that can lead to 'neuromyths'.

Ansari, D., De Smedt, B. and Grabner, R.H. (2012) 'Neuroeducation: a critical overview of an emerging field', *Neuroethics*, 5, pp. 105–117.
Kitchen, W.H. (2021) 'Neuroscience and the Northern Ireland curriculum: 2020, and the warning signs remain', *Journal of Curriculum Studies*, 53(4), pp. 516–530.

Pedagogy > p. 4
Brain plasticity > p. 54
Learning styles > p. 51

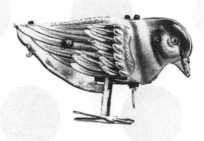

4.5 The Spacing Effect

Learning content is spread across **spaced intervals**, a process that can enhance long-term **retention** of new information. In contrast to spacing is **'cramming'** where learning content is studied intensely for a short period of time before a test. Two forms of spacing are:

- **within session:** spacing of learning content within a learning activity or lesson; and
- **between session:** spacing learning between one lesson and the next.

Despite research evidence that spacing is more effective than cramming, individuals often perceive the opposite to be the case and prefer cramming.

Kornell, N. (2009) 'Optimising learning using flashcards: spacing is more effective than cramming', *Applied Cognitive Psychology*, 23(9), pp. 1297–1317.

Chunking > p. 55
Deep and surface learning > p. 33
Retrieval practice > p. 57
The forgetting curve > p. 56

4.6 Brain Plasticity

Also known as **neuroplasticity**, the brain modifies functions and (re)organises neural pathways in response to **learning** and **experiences**. Plasticity can be affected by age, brain damage and genetic features. The brain retains a capacity for plasticity throughout life, although it tends to decline with age. Engaging in learning (a new language, juggling, o how to play an instrument, for instance) has been argued to positively influence brain plasticity.

The academic literature in this field can be hard to follow for the lay reader; this is compounded by neuroplasticity being a loosely defined term.

Doidge, N. (2007) *The Brain that Changes Itself*. London: Penguin.
Erickson, K.I., Weinstein, A.M. and Lopez, O.L. (2012) 'Physical activity, brain plasticity, and Alzheimer's disease', *Archives of Medical Research*, 43(8), pp. 615–621.
Yuliana, Y. (2020) 'Understanding brain plasticity in learning process', *International Journal of Research in STEM Education*, 2(1), pp. 42–58.

Neuroeducation > p. 52
Non-learning > p. 67

4.7 Chunking

Learning content is organised into a sequence of 'chunks' in order to facilitate students' understanding, memorisation and recall. Chunking what needs to be learned helps the working memory as it receives and **processes** new information.

Chunking derived from George Miller (1956), who proposed that the working memory could hold between five and nine pieces of information at once; however, later studies indicate that the number may be lower.

Miller, G.A. (1956) 'The magical number seven, plus or minus two: some limits on our capacity for processing information', *Psychology Review*, 63(2), pp. 81–97.
Schuessler, J.H. (2017) '"Chunking" semester projects: does it enhance student learning?', *Journal of Higher Education Theory and Practice*, 17(7), pp. 115–120.

Cognitive load > p. 72
Nano-learning > p. 122
Micro-learning > p. 121
The spacing effect > p. 53
Explicit instruction > p. 104

4.8 The Forgetting Curve

A curve that illustrates how individuals forget information over time. Th[e] rate at which information is forgotten may be affected by factors suc[h] as sleep and stress. **Revisiting** and **reviewing** learning content **aids** th[e] **retention** of information. Furthermore, learning content that is **meaningfu[l]** to the individual is retained more easily.

The forgetting curve derives from the work of Hermann Ebbinghau[s] towards the end of the 19th century, whose research involved himself a[s] the **sole participant** and the memorisation of **nonsense syllables**.

Donker, S.C.M., Vorstenbosch, M.A.T.M., Gerhardus, M.J.T. and Thijssen, D.H.J. (2022) 'Retrieval practice and spaced learning: preventing loss of knowledge in Dutch medical sciences students in an ecologically valid setting', *BMC Medical Education*, 22(1), pp. 65–65.
Ebbinghaus, H. (1964) *Memory: A Contribution to Experimental Psychology.* New York: Dover. (The original work was published in 1885.)

The spacing effect > p. 53
Spiral curriculum > p. 38
Cognitive load > p. 72
Meaningful learning > p. 134
Retrieval practice > p. 57

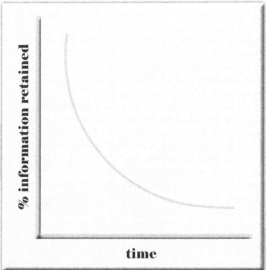

4.9 Retrieval Practice

Students **recall** information previously studied through answering questions or explaining a concept in a **test**. Retrieval activities lead to **improved long-term retention** of knowledge and can foster the memorisation of future new learning content.

Theoretical explanations of these benefits are currently limited (see Minear et al., 2018).

Karpicke, J.D. and Roediger, H.L. (2007) 'Repeated retrieval during learning is the key to long-term retention', *Journal of Memory and Language*, 57(2), pp. 151–162.
Kliegl, O. and Bäuml, K.T. (2021) 'When retrieval practice promotes new learning: the critical role of study material', *Journal of Memory and Language*, 120, article 104253. Available at: https://www.sciencedirect.com/science/article/pii/S0749596X2100036X?via%3Dihub
Minear, M., Coane, J.H., Boland, S.C., Cooney, L.H. and Albat, M. (2018) 'The benefits of retrieval practice depend on item difficulty and intelligence', *Journal of Experimental Psychology: Learning, Memory, and Cognition*, 44(9), pp. 1474–1486.

The spacing effect > p. 53
The forgetting curve > p. 56
Chunking > p. 55
Bloom's taxonomy > p. 26

Chapter 5:

Ways We Learn

5.1 Formal Learning

Learning that is **structured** and **teacher led**, usually taking place in a classroom environment, workshop or webinar. Formal learning takes place within an organised session or programme, and learning objectives are determined by the **teacher**. Learning is focused on the acquisition of established knowledge or information, and tends to lead to some form of **certification** or **credit**.

Formal learning tends to be less flexible and adaptive in meeting the needs of the individual than **informal** learning.

Malcolm, J., Hodkinson, P. and Colley, H. (2003) 'The interrelationships between informal and formal learning', *The Journal of Workplace Learning*, 15(7/8), pp. 313–318.
McGuire, D. and Gubbins, C. (2010) 'The slow death of formal learning: a polemic', *Human Resource Development Review*, 9(3), pp. 249–265.

Explicit instruction > p. 104
Rote learning > p. 132
Didactic teaching > p. 105
Informal learning > p. 62
Active and passive learning > p. 135

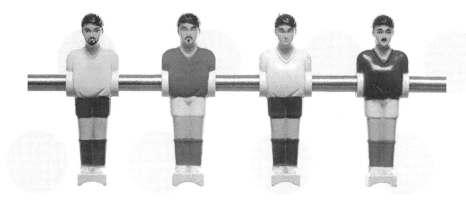

5.2 Informal Learning

Learning that results from work or leisure activities. It has a low degree of planning and structure. It tends to have no set objectives, is non-sequenced, not assessed and such learning is not restricted to certain environments such as the classroom. Informal learning **may involve speaking to a mentor, reading, or watching videos**.

Although this form of learning has widespread support, it has been suggested that informal learning without guidance can lead to individuals feeling directionless.

Malcolm, J., Hodkinson, P. and Colley, H. (2003) 'The interrelationships between informal and formal learning', *The Journal of Workplace Learning*, 15(7/8), pp. 313–318.
McGuire, D. and Gubbins, C. (2010) 'The slow death of formal learning: a polemic', *Human Resource Development Review*, 9(3), pp. 249–265.

Formal learning > p. 61
Incidental learning > p. 64
Coaching and mentoring > p. 87
Heutagogy > p. 22

5.3 Non-formal Learning

Learning characterised as: organised **by educators** (but includes opportunities for student autonomy); taking place **outside** formal educational contexts; **voluntary** in nature (and therefore involves non-mandatory attendance); and often **not leading** to accreditation or certification. Examples include a cooking class or a badminton course.

Researching non-formal learning can be difficult. For instance, it has been argued that students who are research participants are more likely to refer to formal, rather than non-formal, learning.

Eraut, M. (2000) 'Non-formal learning and tacit knowledge in professional work', *British Journal of Educational Psychology*, 70, pp. 113–136.
Nygren, H., Nissinen, K., Hämäläinen, R. and Wever, B. (2019) 'Lifelong learning: formal, non-formal and informal learning in the context of the use of problem-solving skills in technology-rich environments', *British Journal of Educational Technology*, 50(4), pp. 1759–1770.

Formal learning > p. 61
Informal learning > p. 62
Incidental learning > p. 64

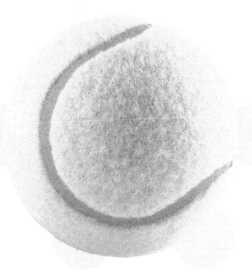

5.4 Incidental and Implicit Learning

 Incidental learning is unintended, unplanned and unstructured. It can occur through engagement in a hobby, social interaction, observing others, or in making mistakes. Such learning is therefore an accidental by-product of engagement in some other activity and tends not to involve conscious reflection. With **implicit learning**, a person is **unaware** that an activity in which they are engaged is incurring changes in their knowledge or skills. The person may later become aware of the learning process that occurred, or not at all.

 As incidental learning is often not recognised as learning by the student or others, it may be difficult to measure or apply the learning elsewhere.

 Kerka, S. (2000) 'Incidental learning', *Trends and Issues*, Alert No. 18. Available at: https://files.eric.ed.gov/fulltext/ED446234.pdf
Marsick, V.J. and Watkins, K.E. (2015) *Informal and Incidental Learning in the Workplace*. London: Routledge.
Simons, P.R.J. and Ruijters, M.C.P. (2004) 'Learning professionals: towards an integrated model', in H.P.A. Boshuizen, R. Bromme and H. Gruber (eds), *Professional Learning: Gaps and Transitions on the Way from Novice to Expert*. Dordrecht: Kluwer Academic.

Formal learning > p. 61
Informal learning > p. 62
Non-formal learning > p. 63

Chapter 6:

Factors Affecting Learning

6.1 Non-learning

Learning can be **hindered** or **blocked** due to issues in one or more of the following three areas:

- **content**: a lack of concentration or a misunderstanding by the student of intended learning may occur due to **insufficient** or **poor explanation** by the teacher. This can lead to mislearning (see 6.2);
- **incentive**: learning may not happen when a student perceives learning content to be in some sense **threatening**;
- **interaction**: circumstances when students experience an objectionable pressure to learn, resulting in **learner resistance**.

Few learning theorists address why learning might not be taking place. Illeris (2007) and Jarvis (2010) are important exceptions to this and make useful contributions in this area.

Illeris, K. (2007) *How We Learn: Learning and Non-learning in School and Beyond.* London: Routledge.
Jarvis, P. (2010) *Adult Education and Lifelong Learning.* 4th edn. London: Routledge.

Mislearning > p. 68
Cognitive load > p. 72
Cognitive dissonance > p. 71
Learning > p. 3

6.2 Mislearning

Learning that does **not** correspond to what was planned or **intended**. Th
may occur due to a **mis**understanding or **lack** of concentration on th
part of the student. A single moment of mislearning can lead to anothe
leading to the risk of a student losing confidence in the subject. On
means to determine whether mislearning is occurring is to ask student
to explain back to the teacher the intended learning of an activity d
lesson. Mislearning can be placed mainly under the **content dimension** d
non-learning (see 6.1).

Determining whether an error has occurred is not always straightforward
For example, students may between them differently interpret a literar
text which has multiple possible interpretations.

Illeris, K. (2007) *How We Learn: Learning and Non-learning in School and Beyond.*
London: Routledge.

Non-learning > p. 67
Cognitive dissonance > p. 71

6.3 Learning Fatigue

Teaching approaches characterised as **repetitive**, **irrelevant**, lacking direct **application**, or **inauthentic** may lead to learning fatigue. Students may become distracted, and attendance may suffer as a result. Learning fatigue can affect students and teachers **alike**.

The term 'learning fatigue' also refers to students' exhaustion resulting from too much screen time from remote teaching and learning.

de Oliveira Kubrusly Sobral, J.B., Lima, D.L.F., Lima Rocha, H.A., de Brito, E.S., Duarte, L.H.G., Bento, L.B.B.B. and Kubrusly, M. (2022) 'Active methodologies association with online learning fatigue among medical students', *BMC Medical Education*, 22(1). Article number 74. Available at: https://bmcmededuc.biomedcentral.com/articles/10.1186/s12909-022-03143-x
Stacey, G., Wilson, C., Reddy, H., Palmer, C., Henderson, J., Little, H. and Bull, H. (2018) 'Diagnosing and treating enquiry based learning fatigue in graduate entry nursing students', *Nurse Education in Practice*, 28, pp. 310–313.

Non-learning > p. 67
Mislearning > p. 68
Formal learning > p. 61

6.4 Dunning-Kruger Effect

 A (novice) individual's **overestimation** of their own **ability** or **knowledg** in a particular discipline, resulting from an **inability** to recognise their ow current level of (in)competence. Novices have poorer **metacognitive** skill than experts to **self-assess** their own competence. As individuals develo their knowledge in the discipline, they also become more aware of th limitations of their own knowledge.

 Dunning and Kruger themselves acknowledge that novices are not alway unaware of their own incompetence. They also identify reasons for th occurrence of this effect other than metacognitive ability, such as tendency for individuals to ignore the abilities of others.

 Kruger, J. and Dunning, D. (1999) 'Unskilled and unaware of it: how difficulties in recognizing one's own incompetence lead to inflated self-assessments', *Journal of Personality and Social Psychology*, 77(6), pp. 1121–1134.

Metacognition > p. 6
Cognitive dissonance > p. 71

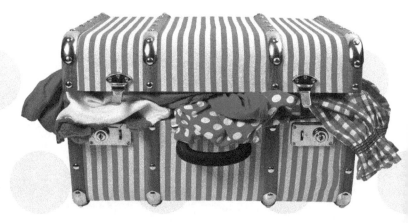

6.5 Cognitive Dissonance

A mental tension that occurs when **individuals hold conflicting cognitions at the same time**.

- **accept** or **reject** the new information;
- add cognitions that **support existing beliefs** or behaviours;
- **reduce the importance** of the new information.

These responses may be seen in students, therefore, when reacting to new information.

It has been argued that while the theory of cognitive dissonance is well established and respected, it has also been characterised **by some (see Vaidis and Bran, 2019)** as difficult to falsify (meaning the claims of the theory are difficult to **be proven wrong**).

Festinger, L. (1957) A *Theory of Cognitive Dissonance*. California: Stanford University Press.
Vaidis, D.C. and Bran, A. (2019) 'Respectable challenges to respectable theory: cognitive dissonance theory requires conceptualization clarification and operational tools', *Frontiers in Psychology*, 10, Article 1189, pp. 1–11.

Metacognition > p. 6
Non-learning > p. 67
Schema > p. 50
Accommodation > p. 16

6.6 Cognitive Load

New information is processed using **working memory**. The capacity o'
working memory is **limited** and it is affected by:

- **intrinsic cognitive load**: the cognitive effort associated with the **inheren'
  nature** of learning content (its level of difficulty or complexity), whicl
  cannot be altered. It is helpful for material to be presented that aligns
  with students' prior knowledge;
- **extraneous cognitive load**: generated by the manner in which learning
  content is **presented**. Extraneous cognitive load should be **minimised**
  through the avoidance of materials with content that is **confusing** o'
  not directly relevant to learning.

A third form, **'germaine cognitive load'**, was disregarded by the author o'
this theory himself, John Sweller, in 2010 (see Garnett, 2020).

de Jong, T. (2010) 'Cognitive load theory, educational research, and instructional design:
some food for thought', *Instructional Science*, 38(2), pp. 105–134.
Garnett, S. (2020) *Cognitive Load Theory: A Handbook for Teachers*. Bancyfelin: Crown
House.
Plass, J.L., Moreno, R. and Brunken, R. (2010) *Cognitive Load Theory*. Cambridge:
Cambridge University Press.

Nano-learning > p. 122
Micro-learning > p. 121
Chunking > p. 55
Schema > p. 50

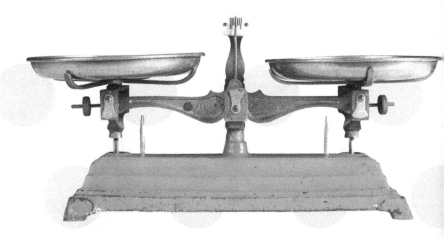

Chapter 7:

Language Learning (Approaches)

7.1 Communicative Approach

Also known as 'communicative language teaching' (CLT), a process that emphasises the acquisition and functional use of authentic and meaningful language through real-life scenarios. The teacher is **facilitator**, and students communicate via interactions with teachers and peers in the **target** language (often in groups or pairs). This may involve role play, pair work or interviews, for instance. CLT has been shown to improve students' language comprehension, language production and fluency.

Language teachers have found that some students resist CLT as it differs from older methods (such as grammar translation) they may be more accustomed to.

Babaeian, A. (2021) 'Approaches to pronunciation instruction in communicative language teaching classrooms', *Journal of Studies in Education*, 11(4), pp. 68–89.
Natsir, M. and Sanjaya, D. (2014) 'Grammar translation method (GTM) versus communicative language teaching (CLT): a review of literature', *International Journal of Education and Literacy Studies*, (2)1, pp. 58–62.
Simion, O.M. (2022) 'The effects of communicative language teaching (CLT) on the post-communicative methodology', *Research and Science Today*, 1, pp. 93–98.

Meaningful learning > p. 134
Active learning > p. 135
The natural approach > p. 80
Grammar translation > p. 76
Facilitation > p. 116

7.2 Grammar-translation Method

Classes are taught in the students' **native language**, and language analysis is prioritised over language use. The focus is on learning **grammatical form** and **translation** from the target language to students' first language. The teacher provides detailed explanations of grammar, and words are **memorised** through the process of translation into the native language.

This method has been considered as monotonous and poor at gaining students' attention. It also side-lines spoken communication and can create anxiety in students who are less confident with studying grammar.

Krashen, S.D. (1987) *Principles and Practice in Second Language Acquisition*. London: Prentice Hall.
Natsir, M. and Sanjaya, D. (2014) 'Grammar translation method (GTM) versus communicative language teaching (CLT): a review of literature', *International Journal of Education and Literacy Studies*, (2)1, pp. 58–62.

Direct method > p. 79
Rote learning > p. 132
Didactic teaching > p. 105

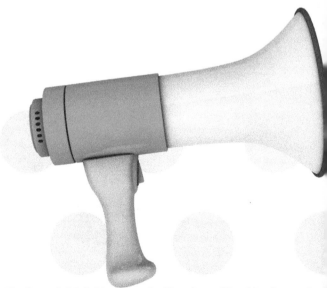

7.3 Dogme

Teaching and learning is centred around **authentic** communication (mostly through **dialogue**), while the use of textbooks is minimised. Language learning that relies heavily on coursebooks is argued to be unsound as they often contain **inauthentic** language, and such materials can become the focus of a lesson, rather than serve to aid to learning. Instead, **students' own lives**, experiences, beliefs and knowledge constitute the principal source or material to draw on for learning. Teachers need to identify and adapt to the individual needs of the students.

This approach may be challenging to implement in large classes where drawing on the ideas of every student could be impractical.

McCabe, D. (2005) 'DOGME', *ELT Journal*, 59(4), pp. 333–335.
Nguyen, N.Q. and Bui Phu, H. (2020) 'The dogme approach: a radical perspective in second language teaching in the post-methods era', *Journal of Language and Education*, 6(3), pp. 173–184.
Thornbury, S. (2000) 'A dogma for EFL', *IATEFL Issues*, 153(2).

Communicative approach > p. 75
Critical pedagogy > p. 23
Humanist education > p. 19
Dialogic pedagogy > p. 113
CLIL > p. 81

7.4 Audio-lingual Method

In reaction to the grammar-translation method (see 7.2), this is a habit-forming approach where spoken language (including **pronunciation** is prioritised. Students repeat dialogues in the target language, with **drilling** and **imitation** used to reinforce structures and aid memorisation. Recordings and visual aids may be used to facilitate the process. Linguistic accuracy is vital and students' correct responses should be positively reinforced.

The audio-lingual method does not embrace errors as a useful part of learning. Further, it has been found that students are often unable to apply the skills learned through this method in real-word communication.

Krashen, S.D. (1987) *Principles and Practice in Second Language Acquisition*. London: Prentice Hall.
Richards, J.C. and Rodgers, T.S. (2001) *Approaches and Methods in Language Teaching*. 2nd edn. Cambridge: Cambridge University Press.

Behaviourism > p. 11
Operant conditioning > p. 13
Rote learning > p. 132
Grammar-translation method > p. 76

7.5 Direct Method

The **target language** is used as the language of instruction and classroom conversation, with **no translations provided** into the students' first language. Learning is **inductive**, meaning students themselves work out language rules, and the focus is on **grammar** and **accuracy**. Realia (real-world objects) or demonstrations may be used help teach concepts or clarify meanings. Teachers ask questions that are interesting and meaningful to their students.

This approach **rarely** leads to **genuinely communicative** discussions, as although there are attempts to make language uses interesting to students the focus will remain on grammar.

Krashen, S.D. (1987) *Principles and Practice in Second Language Acquisition*. London: Prentice Hall.
Richards, J.C. and Rodgers, T.S. (2001) *Approaches and Methods in Language Teaching*. 2nd edn. Cambridge: Cambridge University Press.

Communicative approach > p. 75
Natural approach > p. 80
CLIL > p. 81

7.6 The Natural Approach

The teacher communicates only in the **target** language; students may use their first language or the target language. The focus is on developing communicative skills over language form. Error correction **only** takes place when communication is impeded and in correcting homework. Listening and reading skills are emphasised, as speaking emerges later. Learning is facilitated by a **relaxed** learning environment and may involve realia (authentic materials) such as pictures, magazines or maps, for instance.

It may be of concern that this approach prioritises receptive skills (reading and listening) over productive skills (writing and speaking).

Krashen, S. and Terrell, T. (1983) *The Natural Approach: Language Acquisition in the Classroom.* Oxford: Pergamon.
Richards, J.C. and Rodgers, T.S. (2001) *Approaches and Methods in Language Teaching.* 2nd edn. Cambridge: Cambridge University Press.

The silent way > p. 83
The direct method > p. 79
Communicative approach > p. 75

The Super Quick Guide to Learning Theories and Teaching Approaches

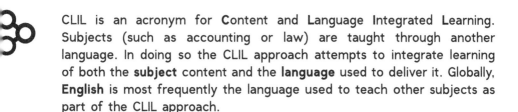

7.7 CLIL

CLIL is an acronym for **C**ontent and **L**anguage **I**ntegrated **L**earning. Subjects (such as accounting or law) are taught through another language. In doing so the CLIL approach attempts to integrate learning of both the **subject** content and the **language** used to deliver it. Globally, **English** is most frequently the language used to teach other subjects as part of the CLIL approach.

The focus in class tends to be on the subject being taught, not on the language being used for instruction by the teacher, particularly when the teacher's level of proficiency in the second language is less strong.

Arnó-Macià, E. and Mancho-Barés, G. (2015) 'The role of content and language in content and language integrated learning (CLIL) at university: challenges and implications for ESP', *English for Specific Purposes*, 37, pp. 63–73.

Direct method > p. 79
The natural approach > p. 80
Cognitive load > p. 72

7.8 Suggestopedia

 This approach emphasises the use of artistic materials within a positive **relaxed** learning environment that facilitates language acquisition. **Group** of 12 students learn through intensive four-hour sessions that involve **extended dialogues** read by the teacher, and students reading along with the text. Other elements include rhythmic breathing, stretching and playing Baroque music. These features are intended to help students relax and reduce their anxiety. Students may practise new language through role play, songs or games.

 Students must acknowledge the absolute **authority** of the teacher. Teachers tend to dominate interactions and do most of the speaking while students mostly listen.

Colliander, H. and Fejes, A. (2021) 'The re-emergence of suggestopedia: teaching a second language to adult migrants in Sweden', Language, Culture, and Curriculum, 34(1), pp. 51–64.
Krashen, S.D. (1987) Principles and Practice in Second Language Acquisition. London: Prentice Hall.

Scaffolding (1) > p. 109
Hierarchy of needs > p. 25

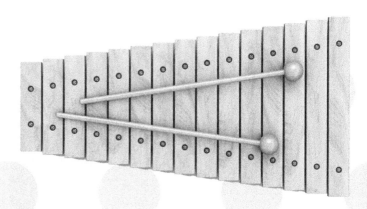

7.9 The Silent Way

This approach emphasises the development of students' independence, autonomy and cooperation. Learning is facilitated when students themselves **discover** and **create**. **Teachers** should be **silent** as much as possible, while students do the talking. The teacher might use gestures, props, or point to wall charts. 'Cuisenaire' rods (coloured, wooden rods) can be used to visually represent a word, structure, or other linguistic feature. Teacher modelling and correction is minimal, while students correct themselves and peers, as well as problem solve, make connections and conceptualise.

This approach could frustrate some students who expect greater verbal input from teachers (such as to correct errors).

Gattegno, C. (1972) *Teaching Foreign Languages in Schools: The Silent Way.* 2nd edn. New York: Educational Solutions.
Richards, J.C. and Rodgers, T.S. (2001) *Approaches and Methods in Language Teaching.* 2nd edn. Cambridge: Cambridge University Press.
Varvel, T. (1979) 'The silent way: panacea or pipedream?', *TESOL Quarterly*, 13(4), pp. 483–494.

Constructivism > p. 15
Active learning > p. 135
Discovery learning > p. 127

7.10 Community Language Learning

This approach draws on **counselling** techniques, with trust and support a key tenets. The teacher functions as counsellor and is non-judgemental empathetic and supportive. Students are clients and members of a **community**, with learning taking place as a **collaborative** endeavour through interactions in this community. Students are positioned in a circle with the teacher on the outside. Example activities include: group presentations o discussion on a topic; recording and transcribing dialogues; and student presenting a drama to the class (with accompanying pictures, music and puppets). Towards the end there is a period of reflection.

Using counselling techniques in this context has been questioned, as ha whether teachers ought to adopt such an approach without training.

Brown, H.D. (1977) 'Some limitations of C-L/CLL models of second language teaching', *TESOL Quarterly*, 11(4), pp. 365–372.
Richards, J.C. and Rodgers, T.S. (2001) *Approaches and Methods in Language Teaching*. 2nd edn. Cambridge: Cambridge University Press.

Humanist education > p. 19
Reflective practice > p. 8
Facilitation > p. 116

Chapter 8: Coaching

8.1 Coaching and Mentoring

Coaching: thought-provoking **questions** are asked by a coach to help individuals achieve their own goals. Coaching can be used in any context and tends to have a set timeframe. Through coaching, the individual owns their own decisions and engages in self-directed learning.

Mentoring: **experienced** in a particular field, mentors share their knowledge, guide and give advice to **less experienced** colleagues. In its simplest terms, while the coach **asks** (questions), the mentor **tells**.

It can be challenging to make progress if changes are needed but an individual does not see any need for change or taking action.

Wilson, C. (2020) *Performance Coaching: A Complete Guide to Best Practice Coaching and Training*. 3rd edn. London: KoganPage.

Zone of proximal development > p. 18
Discovery learning > p. 127
Scaffolding (1) > p. 109

8.2 The GROW Model

 A coaching model that proposes the following process:

- **Goal**: identify and clarify what the coachee wants to achieve.
- **Reality**: discuss the coachee's current situation, including any barrier and previous actions taken.
- **Options**: consider what options are available to achieve the goals.
- **Will**: decide on a course of action, a timeframe and who is account able for what.

The coach is a **facilitator** who helps the other person to identify an choose their own solutions.

 There are variations on what the letters stand for, for example 'O' can als mean 'obstacles', and the 'W' could also mean 'Way forward'.

Whitmore, S.J. (2019) *Coaching for Performance: The Principles and Practice of Coaching and Leadership.* 5th edn. London: Nicholas Brealey.

Zone of proximal development > p. 18
Discovery learning > p. 127
Facilitation > p. 116

8.3 The CLEAR Model

An approach to coaching that suggests the following procedure:

- **Contract**: establish the coachee's desired **outcomes**. Ground rules are also established.
- **Listen**: use active listening, mirroring and reframing to help the coachee understand the situation.
- **Explore**: question, reflect and brainstorm, to develop options regarding the issue.
- **Actions**: the coachee chooses a course of action and the first steps.
- **Review**: discuss actions and reflect on the coaching process itself.

This model differs from the GROW model in its first step, 'Contract', when both the immediate shift needed and the broader goals are addressed.

Hawkins, P. and Smith, N. (2013) *Coaching, Mentoring and Organizational Consultancy: Supervision, Skills and Development.* 2nd edn. Maidenhead: Open University Press.

Zone of proximal development > p. 18
Discovery learning > p. 127
The GROW model > p. 88

8.4 The FUEL Model

This coaching model sets out the following structure:

- **Frame** the conversation. Agree on the purpose, process and desired outcome.
- **Understand** and expand the coachee's awareness of the current situation to help determine the underlying issue.
- **Explore** what success will look like, and paths to achieve this success.
- **Lay out** a plan, including what steps to take, milestones and accountability.

Coaching conversations will often not follow the linear path inferred here (or in other coaching models) and can loop back to previous stages.

Zenger, J.H. and Stinnett, K. (2010) *The Extraordinary Coach: How the Best Leaders Help Others Grow.* New York: McGraw-Hill Education.

Zone of proximal development > p. 18
Discovery learning > p. 127

The Super Quick Guide to Learning Theories and Teaching Approaches

8.5 The OSKAR Model

The following framework is described as enabling **solutions-focused** coaching:

- **Outcome**: establish the objectives of the coachee, today and in the long term.
- **Scaling**: the coachee decides where they are on a scale from 0–10. This facilitates discussion around differences, such as different people's opinions about the issue.
- **Know-how**: reflect on when the objective may have been achieved elsewhere or at another time. Also, consider who and what resources are available to help.
- **Affirm and action**: decide concrete actions that need to be taken.
- **Review**: describe progress towards the objective(s) in subsequent sessions.

The OSKAR model recommends coaches share what impressed them about the coachee during the session.

Jackson, P.Z. and McKergow, M. (2007) *The Solutions Focus: Making Coaching and Change Simple.* 2nd edn. London: Nicholas Brealey International.

Zone of proximal development > p. 18
Discovery learning > p. 127

8.6 Johari Window

A tool that can facilitate self-awareness and interpersonal communication. Four quadrants are identified for reflection:

- **Open**: features known about the person by both themself and others (also called the 'Arena').
- **Hidden**: features known only by the person themselves (this quadrant is also called the 'Façade').
- **Blind spot**: features about the person known by others, but not the person themselves.
- **Unknown**: features about the person not known by themselves or others.

Giving feedback can be challenging as some individuals are very sensitive to hearing feedback about themselves.

Luft, J. and Ingham, H. (1955) *The Johari Window: A Graphic Model for Interpersonal Relations*. Los Angeles: University of California Western Training Lab.

Reflective practice > p. 8
Critical thinking > p. 7
Metacognition > p. 6

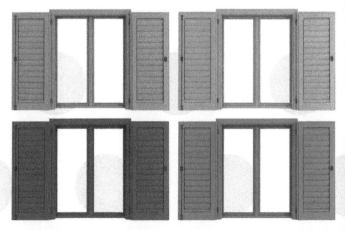

Chapter 9:

Assessing Learning

9.1 Assessment *for* Learning

 Assessment for learning (AFL) is **embedded throughout** the educational process to establish the extent to which each student is learning the **intended** knowledge or skills. The information obtained can be used to **steer** subsequent instruction to **address** remaining **knowledge gaps**. Assessment for learning is often **informal** in nature.

 Note the difference between assessment *for* learning, and **assessment *of* learning**, the latter referring to **summative** (and often **formal**) assessment at the **end of instruction**. There is also **assessment *as* learning**, inferring assessment that is itself a central part of learning.

Harlen, W. (2007) *Assessment of Learning*. London: Sage.
Schuwirth, L.W.T. and Van der Vleuten, C.P.M. (2011) 'Programmatic assessment: from assessment of learning to assessment for learning', *Medical Teacher*, 33(6), pp. 478–485.

Diagnostic assessment > p. 96
Formative and summative assessment > p. 97
Stealth assessment > p. 99

9.2 Diagnostic and Initial Assessment

Diagnostic assessment takes place before instruction around **the start of a topic** or lesson, to establish students' **existing knowledge**, areas of strength and areas for development relating to the topic. This **informs the curriculum and lesson planning**. Diagnostic assessment might involve a quiz, skills test, free writing or discussion.

Initial assessment takes place **prior** to diagnostic assessment and provides information about the students as **individuals**: their **starting point, motivations** and whether there might be any **additional support needs**.

Gravells, A. (2015) *Principles and Practices of Assessment: A Guide for Assessors in the FE and Skills Sector.* 3rd edn. London: Learning Matters.
Lee, Y. and Sawaki, Y. (2009) 'Cognitive diagnosis approaches to language assessment: an overview', *Language Assessment Quarterly*, 6(3), pp. 172–189.

Assessment for learning > p. 95
Formative and summative assessment > p. 97
Stealth assessment > p. 99

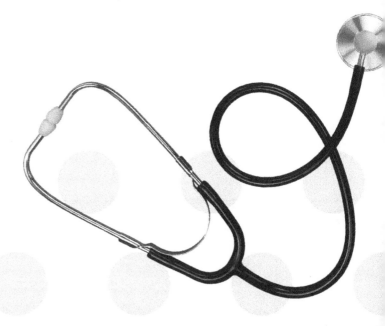

9.3 Formative and Summative Assessment

Formative assessment: activities taking place **during instruction** that provide feedback relating to students' current understanding and where students are having difficulties. This ongoing information can be used to inform future teaching. Such assessment is usually **informal** (the focus is on students' performance rather than grades) and can be **planned or spontaneous**.

Summative assessment: activities taking place **after instruction** that capture what learning has taken place and help establish whether students are ready for the next level. Such assessment is usually **formal** (meaning structured and involving the allocation of grades).

Dixson, D.D. and Worrell, F.C. (2016) 'Formative and summative assessment in the classroom', *Theory into Practice*, 55(2), pp. 153–159.

Assessment for learning > p. 95
Initial and diagnostic assessment > p. 96
Stealth assessment > p. 99
Mastery learning > p. 130

9.4 Self- and Peer Assessment

Self-assessment: students make evaluative judgements about **their own** work (such as a competence, process, or a product) based on specific criteria. This form of assessment can help individuals become **critical, independent** students.

Peer assessment: students judge the **work of peers** based on specific criteria, and give feedback (and possibly grades). This process can foster deep learning, evaluative and reflective skills. Peer assessment can be **anonymised** in instances when students feel uncomfortable giving marks to their peers.

Some literature argues that with peer assessment there may be issues of **validity** relating to the marks given by students to their peers' work due to prejudices, clashes of personality, or loyalties among students. Peer feedback may also be refused by students.

Adachi, C., Tai, J.H. and Dawson, P. (2018) 'Academics' perceptions of the benefits and challenges of self and peer assessment in higher education', *Assessment and Evaluation in Higher Education*, 43(2), pp. 294–306.

Andrade, H.L. (2019) 'A critical review of research on student self-assessment', *Frontiers in Education*, 4(87). Available at: https://www.frontiersin.org/articles/10.3389/feduc.2019.00087/full

Carnell, B. (2016) 'Aiming for autonomy: formative peer assessment in a final-year undergraduate course', *Assessment and Evaluation in Higher Education*, 41(8), pp. 1269–1283.

Assessment for learning > p. 95
Metacognition > p. 6
Critical thinking > p. 7
Deep and surface learning > p. 33

9.5 Stealth Assessment

Assessment that is embedded invisibly into a gaming environment. While playing a game, students engage in tasks that draw on the skills or knowledge being assessed. In assessing students' ongoing interactions with a game, their current knowledge or skills can therefore be determined in any moment. Students' feelings, beliefs and critical thinking may also be obtained through this form of assessment. Unobtrusive stealth assessment can invoke less anxiety in students than traditional forms of assessing learning.

Stealth assessment is open to an **ethical** question of whether students should always be aware of when their knowledge or competencies are being assessed in this way.

Shute, V. and Ventura, M. (2013) *Stealth Assessment: Measuring and Supporting Learning in Video Games.* Cambridge, MA: MIT Press.
Shute, V., Rahimi, S., Smith, G., Ke, F., Almond, R., Dai, C., Kuba, R., Liu, Z., Yang, X. and Sun, C. (2021) 'Maximizing learning without sacrificing the fun: stealth assessment, adaptivity and learning supports in educational games', *Journal of Computer Assisted Learning*, 3(1), pp. 127–141.

Assessment for learning > p. 95
Formative and summative assessment > p. 97
Game-based learning > p. 115
Critical thinking > p. 7

9.6 Feedback and Feedforward

A traditional conceptualisation of **feedback** is one-way evaluativ[e] information transmission where teachers tell students about their **curren[t] performance**. **Feedforward** is future-orientated and involves a teacher-student dialogue, recognising the agency and sense-making of student[s] in understanding how they can improve their **subsequent performance**. Feedforward can take place during a task, so students can mak[e] adjustments in the moment. It can also develop students' goal setting[,] reflection and independence.

It has been argued that effective feedback already incorporates the idea[s] of feedforward. For instance, feedback can also involve dialogue, studen[t] agency and be orientated towards improving future work.

Noon, M.R. and Eyre, E.L.J. (2020) 'A feedforward approach to teaching, learning and assessment in an undergraduate sports science module', *The Journal of Hospitality, Leisure, Sport and Tourism Education*, 27, pp. 1–12.
Reimann, A., Sadlerb, I. and Sambellc, K. (2019) 'What's in a word? Practices associated with "feedforward" in higher education', *Assessment Evaluation in Higher Education*, 44(8)[,] pp. 1279–1290.

Assessment for learning > p. 95
Formative and summative assessment > p. 97
Critical thinking > p. 7
Deep and surface learning > p. 33

Chapter 10:

Teaching Approaches

10.1 Implicit Instruction

The teacher presents information or activities **without specifying** or guiding students as to the intended learning. In language learning, for instance, this approach involves no explicit reference to language **rules** or **forms**; rather, it is intended that students infer rules from examples given. Note the difference with **implicit learning**, where learning is unintentional and unconscious in nature. The opposite approach is **explicit instruction**.

There is little consensus as to whether implicit or explicit instruction leads to more effective learning. Some studies have found that overall neither approach has a clear advantage over the other.

Kapranov, O. (2018) 'The impact of implicit instruction upon the use of English discourse markers in written tasks at the advanced beginners' level of EFL proficiency', *Baltic Journal of English Language, Literature and Culture*, 8, pp. 56–73.
Ke, H., Luo, Y., Piggott, L. and Steinkrauss, R. (2021) 'Long-term effects of explicit versus implicit instruction on EFL writing', *Dutch Journal of Applied Linguistics*, 10, pp. 1–25. Available at: https://dujal.nl/article/view/9361/12389

Explicit instruction > p. 104
Direct method > p. 79
Constructivism > p. 15
Implicit learning > p. 64

10.2 Explicit Instruction

A systematic and scaffolded form of instruction that explicitly draws students' attention to key features of the learning. Chunking is often involved to reduce cognitive load. Opportunities for student responses and teacher feedback are crucial. The opposite approach is **implicit instruction**.

There is little consensus as to whether implicit or explicit instruction leads to more effective learning. Some studies have found that overall neither approach has a clear advantage over the other.

Kapranov, O. (2018) 'The impact of implicit instruction upon the use of English discourse markers in written tasks at the advanced beginners' level of EFL proficiency', *Baltic Journal of English Language, Literature and Culture*, 8, pp. 56–73.
Ke, H., Luo, Y., Piggott, L. and Steinkrauss, R. (2021) 'Long-term effects of explicit versus implicit instruction on EFL writing', *Dutch Journal of Applied Linguistics*, 10, pp. 1–25. Available at: https://dujal.nl/article/view/9361/12389

Implicit instruction > p. 103
Cognitive load > p. 72
Chunking > p. 55
Scaffolding (1) > p. 109

10.3 Didactic Teaching

A **teacher-centred**, **structured** approach, where information is **transmitted** to students through teachers telling students what they need to know. Students are **passive** listeners and recipients of this information. This approach has been traditionally used in higher education lectures with large cohorts of students. The teacher may assess learning through verbal questioning or **summative** assessment tasks.

Contrasting approaches (such as enquiry learning) emphasise that students should be **active** for the most effective learning to take place, as (among other reasons) it facilitates inductive learning, where students themselves work out rules.

Albaradie, R.S. (2018) 'Perception of students and teachers about didactic teaching: a cross-sectional study', *Saudi Journal for Health Sciences*, 7, pp. 107–115.

Formal learning > p. 61
Rote learning > p. 132
Formative and summative assessment > p. 97
Active and passive learning > p. 135

10.4 Differentiation

Recognising that students have **differing** readiness levels, interests, skill and motivations, **all** students' learning needs are met by:

- tailoring teaching strategies according to individuals' learning needs including how learning content is **presented**;
- ensuring a learning **environment** that is safe and challenging for all; and
- involving class activities where **large group**, **small group** and **individual attention** is given.

It can be challenging to reconcile differentiated practice with a need to give standardised grades.

Tomlinson, C.A. (2005) 'Grading and differentiation: paradox or good practice?', *Theory into Practice*, 44(3), pp. 262–269.

Zone of proximal development > p. 18
Personalised learning >
Scaffolding (1) > p. 109
Diagnostic and initial assessment > p. 96

10.5 The Flipped Classroom

A student-centred **blended learning** approach, where new learning content is introduced **digitally** before the main learning session (often with the use of audio or video clips), freeing up class time for students to **actively** question, engage, apply and deepen their understanding of the learning content. This can be facilitated by class activities that are **collaborative** and **problem-based.**

Some studies indicate that this approach does not lead to significant knowledge gains compared to traditional classroom teaching. It has also been argued that the flipped classroom can exacerbate the **digital divide**.

Marks, D.B. (2015) 'Flipping the classroom: turning an instructional methods course upside down', *Journal of College Teaching and Learning*, 12(4), pp. 241–248.
Song, Y. and Kapur, M. (2017) 'How to flip the classroom: "productive failure or traditional flipped classroom" pedagogical design?', *Educational Technology and Society*, 20(1), pp. 292–305.

Active learning > p. 135
Deep and surface learning > p. 33
Problem-based learning > p. 28
Blended and hybrid learning > p. 108
Critical thinking > p. /

10.6 Blended and Hybrid Learning

 Learning that involves a **combination** of **face-to-face** and **technology enabled** instruction. This may involve chatrooms, podcasts and tools for online assessment. Such learning tends to be **synchronous** (students engage at the same time), but it can also be **asynchronous** (students engage at different times) and may involve either **individual** or **group** learning. The terms 'blended' and 'hybrid' are often used interchangeably; however, the latter term has been argued to infer the intentional use of technology to **replace** in-person time (see Saichaie, 2020).

 (Re)designing courses to involve this form of learning can be time consuming. A lack of access to technology may also present a barrier to adopting this approach.

 Madden, A.G., Margulieux, L., Kadel, R.S. and Goel, A.K. (2019) *Blended Learning in Practice: A Guide for Practitioners and Researchers.* Cambridge, MA: MIT Press.
O'Byrne, W.I. and Pytash, K.E. (2015) 'Hybrid and blended learning: modifying pedagogy across path, pace, time, and place', *Journal of Adolescent and Adult Literacy,* 59(2), pp. 137–140.
Saichaie, K. (2020) 'Blended, flipped, and hybrid learning: definitions, developments, and directions', *New Directions for Teaching and Learning,* 2020(164), pp. 95–104.

The flipped classroom > p. 107
Active learning > p. 135

10.7 Scaffolding (1)

Support and **guidance** provided by the teacher during the learning process. Scaffolding occurs within the zone of proximal development (ZPD) and is adjusted according to the **cognitive potential** of the student, and as students' knowledge or proficiency **increases**. Scaffolding can involve **simplifying** tasks or ideas, **demonstrating** processes or **using** modelling. Various forms of scaffolding have been described (see 10.8).

The practicalities of applying scaffolding can be very challenging in contexts where there are large student groups and there is a range of differing support needs.

Smagorinsky, P. (2018) 'Deconflating the ZPD and instructional scaffolding: retranslating and reconceiving the zone of proximal development as the zone of next development', *Learning, Culture and Social Interaction*, 16, pp. 70–75.
Wood, D.J., Bruner, J.S. and Ross, G. (1976) 'The role of tutoring in problem solving', *Journal of Child Psychiatry and Psychology*, 17(2), pp. 89–100.

Constructivism > p. 15
Zone of proximal development > p. 18
Scaffolding (2) > p. 110
Cognitive load > p. 72
Differentiation > p. 106

10.8 Scaffolding (2)

The following forms of scaffolding have been described:

- **hard**: planned in advance and informed by difficulties that student typically have in relation to learning tasks;
- **soft**: calibrated in the moment in response to students' current performance or level of understanding;
- **procedural**: help with using tools and resources;
- **conceptual**: guidance relating to concepts;
- **strategic**: support in tackling problems;
- **metacognitive**: guidance in the thinking process;
- **sensory**: involving the use of realia (real-world objects), imagery models, films or drawings;
- **interactive**: collaborative learning in pairs or groups, with mentors, or online;
- **graphic**: the use of mind maps or graphic organisers (such as Venn diagrams), graphs or timelines.

Jumaat, N.F. and Tasir, Z. (2014) 'Instructional scaffolding in online learning environment: a meta-analysis', *2014 International Conference on Teaching and Learning in Computing and Engineering*, pp. 74–77. Available at: https://www.academia.edu/8370074/Instructional_Scaffolding_in_Online_Learning_Environment_A_Meta_Analysis

Saye, J.W. and Brush, T. (2002) 'Scaffolding critical reasoning about history and social issues in multimedia-supported learning environments', *Educational Technology Research and Development*, 50(3), pp. 77–96.

Walqui, A. (2006) 'Scaffolding instruction for English language learners: a conceptual framework', *International Journal of Bilingual Education and Bilingualism*, 9(2), pp. 159–180.

Constructivism > p. 15
Zone of proximal development > p. 18
Scaffolding (1) > p. 109
Metacognition > p. 6

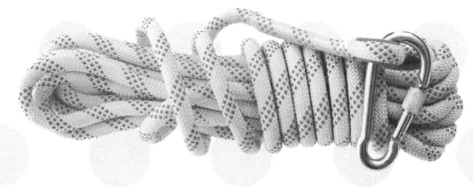

10.9 DIRT

An acronym for **Dedicated Improvement** and **Reflection Time**. Students are given time to **reflect** on and **improve** their work in response to formative **feedback**. DIRT supports students to consider **what** they have learned, **how** they learned and their **progress** towards the learning objectives.

This approach describes regular checkpoints as part of 'assessment **as** learning', meaning assessment itself is central to the process of learning.

Beere, J. (2020) *Independent Thinking on Teaching and Learning: Developing Independence and Resilience in All Teachers and Learners*. Bancyfelin: Independent Thinking Press.
Beere, J. and Gilbert, I. (2012) *The Perfect Ofsted Lesson: Revised and Updated*. Bancyfelin: Independent Thinking Press.

Feedback and feedforward > p. 100
Assessment for learning > p. 95
Scaffolding (1) > p. 109
Metacognition > p. 6
Self- and peer assessment > p. 98

10.10 Co-Teaching

 Two or more educators engage **simultaneously** with a group of student in a learning space. Together these colleagues **plan**, **share** teachir responsibilities and **reflect** on their practice. One may be a specialist a field such as technology, speech therapy, or language teaching. Bot may lead a session, or one might lead while the other helps an individu student. Co-teaching can make differentiated instruction easier and ca lead to improved **pedagogical knowledge** and **student progress**.

 Research on co-teaching is limited, but indicates a range of benefit Communication is important, as is relationship building between the teacher

 Beninghof, A.M. (2020) *Co-teaching that Works: Structures and Strategies For Maximizing Student Learning.* 2nd edn. San Francisco: Jossey-Bass.

Pedagogy > p. 4
Reflective practice > p. 8
Differentiation > p. 106

10.11 Dialogic Pedagogy

A process of learning through **dialogue**, where discussion among people with **differing perspectives** can lead to **new understandings** of a phenomenon. Dialogic pedagogy involves **both teachers and students** talking, and students are encouraged to question the ideas and opinions put forward by teachers, peers and from textbooks. This approach helps students develop critical thinking, reasoning and listening skills.

Dialogic pedagogy (as with other non-didactic approaches) could be difficult for teachers who believe they are the principal owner of knowledge that needs to be **transmitted** to passive (rather than active) students.

Teo, P. (2019) 'Teaching for the 21st century: a case for dialogic pedagogy', *Learning, Culture and Social Interaction*, 21, pp. 170–178.

Active learning > p. 135
Critical thinking > p. 7
Epistemology > p. 5
Constructivism > p. 15
Deep and surface learning > p. 33

10.12 Gamification

The teacher incorporates **game elements** into non-game contexts. Th[e] aim is to increase students' **engagement** and **motivation**, while makin[g] learning **challenging** and **fun**. 'Gamifying' learning activities might involv[e] completing quests, earning rewards, leaderboards, or gaining XP (experiences points).

Points or leaderboards could be considered a shallow means to motiva[te] individuals. It is important that gamified elements are not perceived a[s] superfluous (Armstrong and Landers, 2018).

Armstrong, M.B. and Landers, R.N. (2018) 'Gamification of employee training and development gamification of employee training', *International Journal of Training and Development*, 22(2), pp. 162–169.
Deterding, S., Dixon, D., Khaled, R. and Nacke, L. (2011) 'From game design elements to gamefulness: defining "gamification"', *Proceedings of the 15th International Academic MindTrek Conference*. New York: ACM, pp. 9–15.
Kingsley, T.L. and Grabner Hagen, M.M. (2015) 'Gamification questing to integrate content knowledge, literacy, and 21st-century learning', *Journal of Adolescent and Adult Literacy*, 59(1), pp. 51–61.

Game-based learning > p. 115
Active learning > p. 135
Cooperative learning > p. 120

10.13 Game-based Learning

Gameplay that addresses specific **learning outcomes** through standalone computer games, board games, or real-world **games**. Game-based learning (GBL) has been identified as improving student **motivation** and **engagement**. GBL can be applied to a wide range of subjects, and research indicates that it can facilitate emotional involvement and internal learning motivation.

Excessive competition in gaming can lead to individuals focusing on winning rather than learning; this goal may even lead to cheating (Harviainen et al., 2014).

Harviainen, J.T., Lainema, T. and Saarinen, E. (2014) 'Player-reported impediments to game-based learning', *Transactions of the Digital Games Research Association*, 1(2), pp. 55–83.
Hosseini, H., Hartt, M. and Mostafapour, M. (2019) 'Learning IS child's play: game-based learning in computer science education', *ACM Transactions on Computing Education*, 19(3), Article 22. Available at: https://doi.org/10.1145/3282844

Gamification > p. 114
Active learning > p. 135
Constructivism > p. 15

10.14 Facilitation

The teacher **facilitates** a process where students learn by arriving at their **own understandings** or **solutions**. Three features are key to facilitating learning: being **genuine**, showing **empathy** and having **respect**. The learning environment should feel **safe** and **comfortable** so learners can explore ideas and learn from mistakes.

It has been argued that individuals may not always accept a self-directing role in their own learning. Further, it could be hard to cover a syllabus when the individual has control over their learning.

Regmi, K. (2012) 'A review of teaching methods-lecturing and facilitation in higher education (HE): a summary of the published evidence', *Journal of Effective Teaching*, 12(3) pp. 61–76.
Rogers, C. (1994) *Freedom to Learn*. New York: Prentice Hall.

Humanist education > p. 19
Experiential learning > p. 27
Reflective practice > p. 8
Hierarchy of needs > p. 25

10.15 Enquiry (or, Inquiry) Learning

Students generate and investigate questions, and analyse data relating to a particular subject or topic. Students have opportunities to discuss and reflect on their learning. This process fosters students' curiosity, critical thinking, reflection and the collaborative construction of knowledge. Enquiry learning differs according to the degree of student autonomy, including (from most teacher-centred to most student-centred): **structured**, **controlled**, **guided** and **open** enquiry.

Zion and Mendelovici (2012) suggest that **structured** enquiry does not aid the development of critical and scientific thinking.

Levy, B.L.M., Thomas, E.E., Drago, K. and Rex, L.A. (2013) 'Examining studies of enquiry-based learning in three fields of education: sparking generative conversation', *Journal of Teacher Education*, 64(5), pp. 387–408.

Zion, M. and Mendelovici, R. (2012) 'Moving from structured to open enquiry: challenges and limits', *Science Education International*, 23(4), pp. 383–399.

Constructivism > p. 15
Critical thinking > p. 7
Concept-based enquiry > p. 129
Cooperative learning > p. 120

10.16 Learning Contracts

 A written agreement between the student and their teacher in which the student agrees to undertake particular tasks in a specified timeframe. Learning contracts can help to gradually release responsibility to the student, facilitate self-reflection and support the development of skills such as time management and task prioritisation. Contracts might include **negotiable** and **non-negotiable** elements.

 Some research by Greenwood and McCabe (2008) found a small number of students who described learning contracts as complicated or hard to follow.

 Greenwood, S.C. (2003) 'Contracting revisited: lessons learned in literacy differentiation', *Journal of Adolescent and Adult Literacy*, 46(4), pp. 338–350.
Greenwood, S.C. and McCabe, P.P. (2008) 'How learning contracts motivate students', *Middle School Journal*, 39(5), pp. 13–22.

Active learning > p. 135
Differentiation > p. 106
Self- and peer assessment > p. 98

10.17 Socratic Method

A process of coming to knowledge through **questions** and **dialogue**. The teacher is on the same footing as students and functions as a **facilitator**, who asks probing **open-ended** questions. Giving students sufficient time to process questions and formulate answers is important. Key aims are to explore and question underpinning **beliefs** and **actions**, and stimulate **critical thinking**.

A difficulty in applying this approach is that students may not be willing to answer questions or engage in dialogues. Further, challenging long-held beliefs may create discomfort for some individuals.

Delić, H. and Bećirović, S. (2016) 'Socratic method as an approach to teaching', *European Researcher*, 111(10), pp. 511–517.
Riffel, C. (2014) 'The Socratic method reloaded: how to make it work in large classes?', *Canterbury Law Review*, 20(20), pp. 125–135.

Dialogic pedagogy > p. 113
Critical thinking > p. 7
Epistemology > p. 5
Cognitive dissonance > p. 71

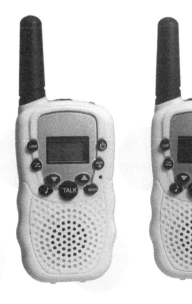

10.18 Cooperative Learning

Students work together in (usually) small **groups**, enabling:

- **positive interdependence**, where every student contributes to the group's learning; and
- **individual accountability**, meaning every student is accountable for their contribution to the work of the group.

There is disagreement relating to the exact features of cooperative learning such as whether cooperative learning should involve extrinsic rewards.

Jolliffe, W. (2007) *Cooperative Learning in the Classroom: Putting it into Practice.* London: Sage.

Active learning > p. 135
Constructivism > p. 15
Enquiry learning > p. 117
Discovery learning > p. 127

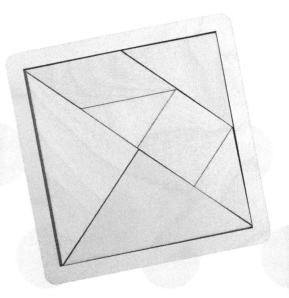

10.19 Micro-learning

Brief, focused learning activities that contain **small chunks** or **units** of information (or, **'microcontent'**). This form of learning aids student **attention**, **retention** of information and can increase student **engagement**. Information is often sourced on, for instance, blog posts or social media (such as Twitter) and tends to focus on one topic. Micro-learning is usually informal and activities can take anything from two minutes up to an hour. **Nano-learning** (see 10.20) can be described as smaller components of micro-learning.

Micro-learning may lead to surface (rather than deep) learning. Also, creating micro-learning content can be very time consuming.

Hug, T., Lindner, M. and Bruck, P.A. (2006) *Microlearning: Emerging Concepts, Practices and Technologies After e-Learning.* Innsbruck: Innsbruck University Press.

Nano-learning > p. 122
Cognitive load > p. 72
Deep and surface learning > p. 33
Chunking > p. 55

10.20 Nano-learning

Learning in a **condensed format** (taking between two and ten minutes) using **small chunks** of **targeted** information that address a **single learning objective**. Learning in small portions helps the retention of new information and may involve a video, quiz, text, social media, or infographics. Cited as particularly useful as a **refresher task** in corporate contexts, nano-learning can reduce cognitive (over)load. Nano-learning breaks down **micro-learning** objectives into smaller learning points.

Individualised feedback may be hard to give following nano-learning activities.

Gramming, A.K., Ejemyr, E. and Thunell, E. (2019) 'Implementing nano-learning in the law firm', *Legal Information Management*, 19(4), pp. 241–246.
Khlaif, Z. and Salha, S. (2021) 'Using TikTok in education: a form of micro-learning or nano-learning?', *Interdisciplinary Journal of Virtual Learning in Medical Sciences*, 12(3) pp. 213–218.

Micro-learning > p. 121
Chunking > p. 55
Cognitive load > p. 72

10.21 Outdoor Learning

Experiential learning that takes place in **outdoor** environments. This approach encompasses numerous learning activities, for instance: making a house for a hedgehog; using trigonometry to estimate the height of a tree; and creating artwork using sticks, leaves and pine needles (see Bushnell, 2020). Outdoor learning can foster students' creativity, teamwork, leadership skills and independence.

An important consideration is that of health and safety concerns relating to slippery surfaces, plants, animals and the weather.

Bushnell, A. (2020) *Outdoor Learning*. London: Bloomsbury Education.
Davies, R. and Hamilton, P. (2018) 'Assessing learning in the early years' outdoor classroom: examining challenges in practice', *Education* 3-13, 46(1), pp. 117–129.

Active learning > p. 135
Experiential learning > p. 27
Play-based learning > p. 32

10.22 Maker Education

 Relating predominantly to **STEM** (meaning science, technology, engineering and maths) subjects, an **active** learning approach of making things that aid the development of students' interests, identity and knowledge. Students (or, 'makers') engage in **hands-on**, **project-based** activities that explore concepts and phenomena such as, for example, motion and magnetism. 'Maker**spaces**' are places that contain various **materials** for making and enable collaborative learning.

 In some contexts there may be limited availability of makerspaces and materials for making.

 Hsu, Y., Baldwin, S. and Ching, Y. (2017) 'Learning through making and maker education', *TechTrends*, 61(6), pp. 589–594.

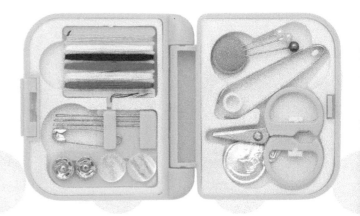

10.23 Personalised Learning

Learning that is tailored to each student's individual needs and interests. Students **actively** address **authentic problems** at their own pace to meet outcomes that are meaningful and relevant. Students are involved in the process of goal-setting and in making decisions relating to their own learning. Learning technologies are often used to facilitate personalised learning.

Planning for and enacting personalised learning for every student can be time consuming and challenging, particularly with large student groups.

Hughey, J. (2020) 'Individual personalized learning', *Educational Considerations*, 46(2), pp. 1–8. Available at: https://newprairiepress.org/cgi/viewcontent.cgi?article=2237 andcontext=edconsiderations

Active learning > p. 135
Meaningful learning > p. 134
Humanist education > p. 19
Differentiation > p. 106
Scaffolding (1) > p. 109

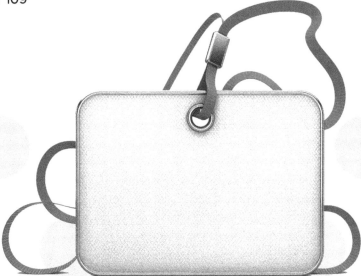

10.24 Nine Events of Instruction

Nine events (or steps) that provide a **framework** for learning. The teacher **designs** and **manages** the learning process. These nine events occur in three phases: **engagement**, **delivery** and **assessment**.
Engagement: gain students' attention, give objectives, stimulate recall of prior learning.
Delivery: present learning content, provide guidance to students, elicit performance (meaning students demonstrate understanding through practice activities).
Assessment: provide feedback, assess performance, enhance retention and facilitate knowledge transfer (students apply learning elsewhere).

This systematic approach may limit students' ability to explore and guide their own learning.

Gagne, R.M. (1985) *The Conditions of Learning and Theory of Instruction.* 4th edn. New York: Holt, Rinehart and Winston.

Behaviourism > p. 11
Formal learning > p. 61
Assessment for learning > p. 95

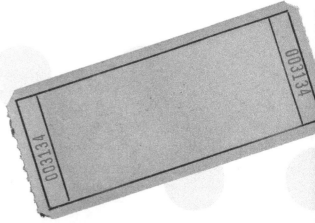

10.25 Discovery Learning

Discovery learning emphasises learning by doing and problem solving, rather than passively receiving new information. Discovery learning encourages a culture of **open-mindedness**, **questioning** and **collaboration**. Students draw on their own **experiences** and **existing knowledge** to find things out themselves. There are differing forms of discovery learning, including:

- **pure discovery**: students engage in unstructured exploration with maximum freedom and little or no guidance;
- **guided discovery**: students receive some form of support in addressing a problem, through hints, coaching or feedback, for example.

It has been argued that with a pure discovery approach students may fail to identify or learn the rule or principle that is intended as an outcome.

Bruner, J.S. (1961) 'The act of discovery', *Harvard Educational Review*, 31, pp. 21–32.
Mayer, R.E. (2004) 'Should there be a three-strikes rule against pure discovery learning? The case for guided methods of instruction', *American Psychologist*, 59(1), pp. 14–19.

Enquiry learning > p. 117
Constructivism > p. 15
Active learning > p. 135
Problem-based learning > p. 28
Active and passive learning > p. 135

10.26 Concept-based Learning

Students learn **concepts** that are **transferable** within and across disciplines. Concept-based learning involves students making **connections** and identifying **patterns** in learning content. Teaching concepts (or 'big ideas') can aid student **engagement** and **agency**; it also helps students understand the relevance of what they are learning.

Also see **concept-based enquiry** (section 10.27), an approach that merges concept-based learning and enquiry learning.

Marschall, C. and French, R. (2018) *Concept-based Enquiry in Action: Strategies to Promote Transferable Understanding.* Thousand Oaks, CA: Corwin Press.

Enquiry learning > p. 117
Concept-based enquiry > p. 129
Critical thinking > p. 7
Deep and surface learning > p. 33
Constructivism > p. 15

10.27 Concept-based Enquiry

Drawing from both **enquiry** learning and **concept-based** learning, concept-based enquiry is a form of enquiry learning in which teachers support their students to articulate **transferable**, **conceptual** understandings, while developing **enquiry skills**.

- The focus of concept-based learning is on learning **concepts** that are **transferable** within and across disciplines (see 10.26).
- Enquiry learning is driven by students' investigation of questions, discussion and reflection on learning (see 10.15).

The teacher may have to address the issue of individuals who may be less willing to participate in this student-led approach.

Marschall, C. and French, R. (2018) *Concept-based Enquiry in Action: Strategies to Promote Transferable Understanding.* Thousand Oaks, CA: Corwin Press.

Enquiry learning > p. 117
Concept-based learning > p. 128
Critical thinking > p. 7
Deep and surface learning > p. 33
Constructivism > p. 15

10.28 Mastery Learning

Students must achieve a certain level of knowledge (or 'mastery') at one stage before moving on to the next stage. For this to occur, there need to be: clear learning **objectives** at each stage; suitable diagnostic and formative **assessments**; and sufficient **time** to master the learning. Learning units need to be **manageable** and **ordered** by increasing **difficulty**. Should a student not pass an assessment, additional support is provided in advance of a further assessment.

As most students are required to master (the same) specified level at each stage, a challenge can be that students will sometimes require different amounts of time and attention to achieve mastery.

Bloom, B.S. (1971) *Mastery Learning*. New York: Holt, Rinehart and Winston.
Carroll, J.B. (1963) 'A model of school learning', *Teachers College Record*, 64(8), pp. 723–733.

Surface and deep learning > p. 33
Diagnostic and initial assessment > p. 96
Formative and summative assessment > p. 97
Chunking > p. 55

10.29 Just-in-time Learning

A dynamic form of learning that takes place at the precise **time and place** it is needed by individuals, often involving the use of **educational technologies**. Just-in-time learning usually addresses a **single**, **specific** learning objective and involves small pieces of learning content. This form of learning tends to be informal and student-driven, and can lead to strong engagement and knowledge **retention**.

A potential concern is that an individual may **not be aware** of a gap in their knowledge that needs to be addressed, so may not seek such learning.

Brandenburg, D.C. and Ellinger, A.D. (2003) 'The future: just-in-time learning expectations and potential implications for human resource development', *Advances in Developing Human Resources*, 5(3), pp. 308–320.

Micro-learning > p. 121
Nano-learning > p. 122
Chunking > p. 55
Deep and surface learning > p. 33
Informal learning > p. 62

10.30 Rote Learning

Learning takes places through **repetition** or **drilling** that leads to **memorisation**. The focus therefore is less on comprehension or application of learning content. This approach is often applied when mastering **elementary aspects** within particular fields, such as multiplication in maths. Tools such as **flashcards** are sometimes used in the process.

Rote learning has been argued to inhibit a deeper understanding of concepts and information, and not stimulate the development of students' critical thinking or metacognition. Others, however, defend rote learning as an effective approach in obtaining base knowledge.

Ahmed, A. and Ahmad, N. (2017) 'Comparative analysis of rote learning on high and low achievers in graduate and undergraduate programs', *Journal of Education and Educational Development*, 4(1), pp. 111–129.
Nesbitt, D. (2009) 'Achieving unconscious recall of kanji: can rote learning help?', *New Zealand Studies in Applied Linguistics*, 15(2), pp. 61–73.

Formal learning > p. 61
Explicit instruction > p. 104
Deep and surface learning > p. 33
Active and passive learning > p. 135

10.31 Growth Mindset

Students with a '**fixed** mindset' understand ability to be **innate** and **unchangeable**. Individuals with a '**growth mindset**' believe they can acquire and develop abilities through **effort**; challenges and failures are opportunities to **learn and grow**. The use of specific **language** is used, such as: 'I can't do this **yet**.' The teacher can foster a growth mindset by emphasising **hard work** and giving **praise** for the efforts their students make.

It has been noted that academic outcomes are not accounted for solely by the individual having a fixed or growth mindset (see Corradi et al., 2018).

Corradi, D., Nicolaï, J. and Levrau, F. (2018) 'Growth mindset and its predictive validity: do migration background and academic validation matter?', *Higher Education*, 77(3), pp. 491–504.
Dweck, C.S. (2012) *Mindset: How You Can Fulfil Your Potential*. London: Robinson.

Active learning > p. 135
Non-learning > p. 67
Self- and peer assessment > p. 98

10.32 Meaningful Learning

 Learning characterised as authentic, relevant, significant and valued by students themselves. Meaning is constructed by each student and new information is related to existing knowledge. 'Meaningful' learning occurs when new knowledge challenges or builds on prior understandings. This form of learning is enabled in contexts with high student engagement and agency, in contrast to rote learning.

 Such learning can lead to discomfort as pre-existing knowledge or beliefs are challenged by new information.

Jarvis, P. (1987) 'Meaningful and meaningless experience: towards an analysis of learning from life', *Adult Education Quarterly*, 37(3), pp. 164–172.
Kostiainen, E., Ukskoski, T., Ruohotie-Lyhty, M., Kauppinen, M., Kainulainen, J. and Mäkinen, T. (2018) 'Meaningful learning in teacher education', *Teaching and Teacher Education*, 71, pp. 66–77.

Constructivism > p. 15
Deep and surface learning > p. 33
Critical thinking > p. 7
Accommodation > p. 16
Humanist education > p. 19
Cognitive dissonance > p. 71

10.33 Active and Passive Learning

With **active learning** individuals **actively participate** in learning activities, meaning they are doing more than just listening to the teacher. **Inductive** learning is often involved, where students engage in **knowledge construction** to work out themselves the rules and principles in learning content. This approach can therefore help develop reflection and metacognition. Students may also have some **control** over the learning process itself. **Passive learning** is a teacher-centred approach where the teacher transmits information to students, who passively listen and rarely ask questions.

Although active learning is widely advocated, there may be occasions when passive learning is also effective. For instance, lectures involving passive learning have the potential to stimulate ideas and lead to new thinking (Postholm, 2012).

Bell, B.S. and Kozlowski, S.W.J. (2008) 'Active learning: effects of core training design elements on self-regulatory processes, learning, and adaptability', *Journal of Applied Psychology*, 93, pp. 296–316.
Postholm, M.B. (2012) 'Teachers' professional development: a theoretical review', *Education Research*, 54(4), pp. 405–429.

Constructivism > p. 15
Cognitivism > p. 14
Behaviourism > p. 11
Epistemology > p. 5
Metacognition > p. 6

Index of Entries